AND THE POOR GET WELFARE

AND THE POOR GET WELFARE

The Ethics of Poverty in the United States

Warren R. Copeland

ABINGDON PRESS
Nashville

in cooperation with
THE CHURCHES' CENTER FOR THEOLOGY
AND PUBLIC POLICY
Washington, D.C.

AND THE POOR GET WELFARE:
THE ETHICS OF POVERTY IN THE UNITED STATES

Library of Congress Cataloging-in-Publication Data

Copeland, Warren, R.
    And the poor get welfare : the ethics of poverty in the United States / Warren R. Copeland.
        p. cm.
    Includes bibliographical references.
    ISBN 0-687-01386-0 (pbk.)
    1. Public welfare—United States—Moral and ethical aspects.   2. Poverty—United States—Moral and ethical aspects.   3. Social ethics—United States.   I. Churches' Center for Theology and Public Policy (Washington, D.C.)   II. Title.
HV95.C649   1994   94-9873
362.5'0973—dc20   CIP

94 95 96 97 98 99 00 01 02 03 — 10 9 8 7 6 5 4 3 2 1

MANUFACTURED IN THE UNITED STATES OF AMERICA

To Vera, Rush, and Delpha Copeland,
who taught me the meaning of family, work, and love

CONTENTS

ACKNOWLEDGMENTS

Some twenty-five years ago I was first introduced to the public policy issues associated with poverty in the United States in a course taught by Ed Becker at Christian Theological Seminary (CTS). At about the same time, also at CTS, I was introduced to process theology by Clark Williamson. Thus began my efforts to bring the two into dialogue.

I took these interests to the University of Chicago where they became the subject of my dissertation, a study of the Nixon effort to reform the welfare system. In my first course at Chicago, Al Pitcher introduced me to the analytic framework that organizes my reading of alternative views of poverty, which follows; later he forced me to read Tillich's third volume more closely than I thought I could and advised my dissertation.

Most influential in my education at Chicago was Alan Anderson, who introduced me to Aristotle, Arendt, and Dewey, expanded my knowledge of Whitehead, and insisted that I think for myself. Perhaps most importantly, Alan organized the conversation that has become the Social Ethics Seminar, my primary circle of influence and criticism. The central elements of this volume were presented to the Social Ethics Seminar where they received valuable criticism.

Two members of the Seminar particularly influenced important revisions of this text. George Pickering helped me be much more direct about my theological position while keeping the language as simple as possible. Roger Hatch took the time to read the entire text and give immeasurable help in organizing the last third of the book much more clearly.

The sabbatical program of Wittenberg University allowed me to dedicate most of three spring terms to researching and writing this volume. Jeff Ankrom of the Wittenberg Economics Department is my primary local sounding board, and Jim Huffman of the Wittenberg History Department read part of the manuscript. Gretchen Baur, my student assistant, did a lot of footwork and copying. Rosie Burley, Wittenberg's faculty secretary, typed the manuscript and revisions with her usual competence and good humor.

The flexibility of the course offerings in the Religion Department at Wittenberg allowed me to teach the essential elements of this work in my Belief and Action course. I have yet to find any better way to make sure I have read a book carefully than to teach it to others. Certainly the students in Belief and Action tested and added to my understanding of the books we read together.

Rex Matthews of Abingdon Press first suggested that this volume might fit in the Churches' Center for Theology and Public Policy (CCTPP) series and provided supportive words along the way. Jim Nash of the CCTPP provided helpful criticism of the first draft. Ulrike Guthrie of Abingdon Press not only made helpful specific suggestions but also raised the more basic issues that led to important revisions in the final text.

It is customary for authors to thank their spouses for their loving support during the writing of a book, and I certainly owe such gratitude to Clara Coolman Copeland. However, Clara has played a much more influential role in the content of this work. As an urban kindergarten teacher who gets close to her children and their families, she has become my primary source of information about the lived experience of people who do not have much money.

Scott and Karen Copeland, our son and daughter, were college students during the writing of this book. They have reminded me of just how much struggle is involved in becoming adults and just how much our adult selves are rooted in our childhoods, for good and ill.

I have dedicated this book to three of my parents. My mother, Vera Copeland, was the child of a single-parent family. My father, Rush Copeland, was the child of a family that disintegrated in his youth. Both were poor before and after they found each other. Yet, they lived and taught me the deepest meaning of a loving family and hard work. Delpha Copeland married Dad in his later years and loved him through some very difficult times. I am their child and student.

CHAPTER ONE

AND THE POOR GET POORER
(AND YOUNGER)

S hawn confirms most of the stereotypes people have about welfare recipients. He is quite willing to let other people provide him with those things he needs in life. He would much rather play around with his friends than work. He puts his short-term fun ahead of long-term plans, especially ones that require sacrifice in the short run. He has big dreams about what he wants to be someday but no real idea of how to make them come true. Deep inside is quite a bit of anger that comes out every now and then, getting him in trouble with the authorities. The one way that Shawn is typical of welfare recipients which does not fit the usual stereotype is that Shawn is six years old. About two-thirds of the recipients of Aid to Families with Dependent Children (AFDC), what most Americans mean by welfare, are children like Shawn.[1]

What I did not describe about Shawn is the twinkle in his eye when he is having fun. I did not mention how much he loves to explore new ideas and to learn about how a new toy or game works. I did not tell about how he freely celebrates when his sister does well in a game, even if he loses as a result, or how he settles down to listen to a book read to him at bedtime or how genuinely he hugs someone who has shown him a little love. All in all, Shawn is like most kids his age. And yet he is not. Shawn's father has served time in jail a couple of times and has now disappeared. His mother does not have the money to buy him the things he sees on television. He has waited and waited and waited with his mother and sister at the Salvation Army in order to get a Christmas present.[2] He goes to a school where a majority of the other children are as poor as he. Most important, Shawn himself is likely to grow up to be poor.

One of the most difficult problems for people who try to address issues of social ethics is well illustrated by Shawn. If we stress the difficulty of his life, for instance the likelihood that he will grow up to be poor, we transform him from a real human being into a helpless victim. If we are not careful, we develop a well-meaning but paternalistic attitude toward kids like Shawn that ignores or undermines their integrity. Too often this is the attitude that marks charity and, in spite of the good intentions of the givers, makes it difficult for recipients of it to retain the self-respect essential to human dignity. From the point of view of this attitude, Shawn is a poor little kid who needs help rather than the tough, caring, inquisitive, and spunky little guy he is and must remain if he is to thrive or even to survive. Seeing Shawn as only a victim makes it impossible for us to see him as our fellow human being and citizen. Moreover, if Shawn is treated only as a victim it can make it impossible for him to see himself as just as worthwhile as other people.[3]

One simple way to escape this danger of paternalism is to ignore Shawn's problems and to act as though his life is just like those of children who are not poor. This solution is particularly attractive to Americans because we have been reared on stories about poor people who have risen to great success and wealth through heroic efforts. If these people have made it, so can Shawn. And of course it may be true. Perhaps Shawn will channel his anger behind his inquisitiveness and direct them in a lawful way and become a great success. It is much more likely, however, that Shawn's situation will keep him from being a successful adult. While we parents who are not poor may refuse to accept this reality intellectually, we act upon it. Given the choice, we are clear we would not want our own children to grow up in Shawn's situation. To deny this reality is to be dishonest with ourselves and unfair to Shawn.

What, then, are we to do? In the long run, we shall develop an understanding of human reality that helps us think about the relation between individual and community in a way which recognizes the power of social relations while preserving individual integrity and responsibility.[4] But the issue is much more immediate at this point. How do we relate to Shawn's life story in an honest but sensitive way? Put more concretely, how do we recognize the real pain and tough odds that Shawn faces without dehumanizing him? For now, two guidelines will have to do. First, we need to suspend immediate judgments and try to imagine what life is really like for Shawn. This is harder than it may sound. It is not enough to put ourselves as we are presently formed in his place; rather we must try to picture what we ourselves would be if we had lived Shawn's life up to this point. How would we act if we had seen and felt all that Shawn has seen and felt? Having tried to do this, we must recognize that we finally cannot know what Shawn's life is like, and so we should follow the second guideline, which is to respect his right to speak for himself and to live his own life.

Actually, most of us would find it relatively easy to be both empathetic and respectful of Shawn. After all, he is only six years old. He is hardly to blame for his poverty. It is not surprising that the most effective advocate for the poor these days is the Children's Defense Fund, which frames all of the problems of poverty in terms of what they mean for children.[5] The only trouble with this approach is that nearly all poor children live with poor adults. This seems like an obvious truth, and yet it nearly always escapes the most vocal critics of welfare. Every radio talk show host in America knows that listeners agree strongly with calls for punishing recipients who will not work, have more children while on welfare, or make a little money they do not report to welfare officials. "Cut off her welfare!" is the nearly unanimous cry. Yet these same listeners express great sympathy for the poor children, especially if they are relatively young, who live with and are dependent upon that adult welfare recipient. Our inability to reconcile our nearly unanimous condemnation of welfare recipients with our equally unanimous sympathy for their children is but one of our fundamental moral ambiguities about poverty, which we must look squarely in the face if we are to think creatively about welfare policy.[6]

In Shawn's case, he lives with his mother, Marie. His father has been in and out of his life because he served some short time in jail twice and has separated from Shawn's mother a number of times. Marie has her own life story. Born too poor and married too young, she had Shawn before her husband Stan began to come and go; Shawn's younger sister Jennifer was conceived during one of their brief reconciliations. Marie is bright enough to have earned a General Education Degree (GED), a high school diploma by examination. She has started a practical nursing program a number of times but various family crises have intervened each time. Marie also has a number of personal problems. Some she might have even if she had not been born poor; however, some clearly were caused or made worse by her poverty. In any event when she was Shawn's age, she was just as tough, sensitive, inquisitive, and spunky as he is now.

Why would most Americans not blame Shawn at all for his poverty and yet hold Marie responsible for hers, and probably for Shawn's too? Somewhere between Shawn's age six and Marie's age twenty-three, we begin to hold people responsible for their lives because we believe their poverty is the result of choice rather than the accident of birth. At just what age does that scale tip? When Marie was Shawn's age, we could predict that she was likely to grow up to be poor. Why is it her fault? The odds are strong that Shawn will grow up to be poor. If he does, will it be his fault? Our answers to these questions imply a lot about what we believe to be the relative power of individual choice and of social forces. These answers may have more to say about what we who are not poor hope and believe about our own lives than about Shawn or Marie. If Marie is not to blame for her economic failure, perhaps we do not deserve credit for our economic success.[7]

POVERTY AND WELFARE FACTS[8]

It is true, however, that Marie has not taken a permanent full-time job, that she had a child while she was on welfare, that she has made some money from time to time that she did not report to the welfare department, and that she did let Stan return home more than once without telling the welfare department. Does this make her a lazy, child-breeding, welfare cheat? Perhaps. It also means she is a human being who has attempted, as best she can, to hold her family together through tough times. In any event, in one respect she certainly is the typical recipient of AFDC.[9] The vast majority of welfare recipients are young women with one or two children they are trying to raise by themselves. Once they get a bit older and their children go to day care or school, most of them will leave welfare.

In many important ways Shawn and Marie are typical not just of welfare recipients but increasingly of poor people generally. One-third of all female-headed households live in poverty; one-half of nonwhite female-headed households do. For young women the numbers are even more dramatic. Two-thirds of all households headed by women aged fifteen to twenty-four years live in poverty; three-fourths of nonwhite families of the same sort do. In 1990, children under eighteen years of age were more likely to be poor than any other age group. Twenty percent of all children, 45 percent of African American children, live in poverty. This is an increase from 15 percent in 1970. Government programs have reduced dramatically the poverty rate among the elderly during the same period of time. Clearly, poverty for female-headed households and for children go together. Children living in such households are five times more likely to be poor than families with two parents; half of poor children live in female-headed households. As far as poverty in the United States is concerned, women and children do come first.

Marie and Shawn are typical in one other way: they are white. If we are to discuss poverty and welfare policy seriously, we must learn at least some very basic statistical principles. Here is a good place to begin. African Americans are about three times as likely to be poor as white Americans are. At the same time, a majority of Americans who are poor or on welfare are white. Both of these statements are true, primarily because African Americans make up only about one-eighth of the American population (12.1 percent in 1990). So, even though a much larger portion of the African American population is poor, that is still a smaller number of people than the much smaller portion of white Americans who are poor relative to the overall white population. Whenever people refer to percentages or fractions, we must ask what the size of the whole is. To sum up, the commonly held stereotype of a welfare recipient is an African American mother of a large number of children who has lived on welfare for years. In fact, a majority of the women who head welfare families are young, white, have only one or two children, and will leave welfare within a year or two.

In other important ways, Marie is not typical of poor Americans. Most poor Americans are not welfare recipients; about 60 percent of all poor families have at least one person who is employed. We need only reflect for a bit about low-wage jobs to see the problem. A minimum-wage job may produce enough income after deductions to keep an individual out of poverty, but it will not do so for a family. Since such jobs seldom provide fringe benefits, especially health care, they often do not even compete well with welfare in states with relatively high benefits. Poor families have tried to deal with low wages in the same way other American families have, by both parents working. When no family member is able to hold a better-paying job or two people do not work full time, the family remains poor. Until recently, about half of the states only provided some form of General Assistance to families with two parents with benefits typically much lower than AFDC. Only when the father left did the family qualify for AFDC. The latest changes in the federal law make it no longer necessary for a parent to leave.[10]

WHAT IS POVERTY?

In all of the previous discussion of the statistics of poverty, I have been using the official definition of poverty by the United States government. This is itself controversial. That definition was developed in a deceptively simple way in the early sixties by a Kennedy administration employee named Mollie Orshansky.[11] She began with the result of a Department of Agriculture survey, which showed that the average low-income American family spent one-third of their income on food. Then, she asked what a minimal family food budget would be. The Department of Agriculture actually had priced two such food budgets—the "low cost" budget, which would provide minimum nutrition for an extended period of time, and the "economy" budget, which would provide an adequate emergency diet only for a limited time. She simply multiplied this minimal food budget by three to establish the minimum total budget—that is, the poverty level. In 1964 the "low cost" food budget indicated a poverty level for a family of four of nearly $4,000 and the "economy" food budget indicated one of just over $3,000. A political decision was made to go with the lower number because it could not be criticized as too liberal, and it still produced numbers justifying a War on Poverty that could be won.

That official poverty figure has remained debatable ever since. Conservatives argue that in deciding who falls below it, benefits which do not come in cash—housing, medical care, food stamps, and such—are not counted. They also suggest that adjusting it for inflation by using the Consumer Price Index (which results in an estimated poverty level of $14,000 for a family of four in 1993) is misleading because it is based on things poor people do not usually do, such as buy homes.[12] Liberals point out that the poverty level was based initially on an emergency food budget that the Department of Agriculture itself considers inadequate. Furthermore, they point out that mere survival is hardly a generous target.[13] A family of four with an income of $14,500, and so not officially poor, is not living appreciatively better than the officially poor one with an income of $13,500. Neither lives at the level assumed by advertising on television. More important, most families who live just above the poverty level lack health insurance and job security. They are only one major illness, accident, or layoff away from poverty.

This debate over where poverty begins and ends can go on forever and is finally pointless. Poverty is essentially a social function of a given society.[14] How much income does it take to be a full participant in a particular society? Certainly most families defined as poor and living as such in the United States have higher incomes than most people in many other countries. What an official poverty level does is allow us to compare various historical points and to determine in what directions the trends are running. Beyond the debate over the official definitions of poverty, most experts of various political persuasions agree that the trends in recent American poverty statistics are quite troubling.

TROUBLING TRENDS IN POVERTY[15]

Three particular trends deserve mention. First of all, poverty in America steadily declined from 1960 when it was 22.2 percent for the general population until 1972 when it stood at 11.1 percent. Since 1972 the poverty rate has edged upward again, pushing 14 percent. Since the poverty rate varies with the ups and downs of the general economy, the resurgence of poverty can be made to look more or less dramatic depending on which years are chosen for comparison, but the long-term trend of slow but steady increase seems clear. Such a trend is particularly difficult to accept in a nation that prides itself on providing opportunity. This is especially true because the very well off were doing even better during the same period of time. Prior to 1982, the income of the bottom one-fifth was growing more quickly than was that of the top one-fifth. After 1982, that trend reversed and the income of the top one-fifth grew significantly faster than that of the bottom one-fifth. In sum, the rich got richer in the eighties even as poverty increased.

The second trend in the statistics is that the poor in America are getting younger each year. In part this is a result of positive changes. Government programs have virtually eliminated poverty among the elderly, a group where it traditionally ran high. Nearly all of the elderly are now covered by social security and Medicare or comparable programs. Usually those who are not, receive Supplemental Security Income (SSI), which is federally funded. Nearly all of these federally funded basic support programs for the elderly include provisions for automatic cost-of-living adjustments to keep pace with inflation. While many elderly persons continue to live on very limited income, very few now fall below the official poverty level.

At the same time, the increase in single-parent families made more and more children vulnerable to poverty. Since the programs (primarily AFDC and Medicaid) that serve children are funded in part by state and local governments, they were more vulnerable than the federally funded programs for the elderly. When inflation struck in the late seventies few states kept pace, so the buying power of the grants shrank, typically by more than a third. With slow economic growth in the eighties, states saw their revenues decline. Faced with the requirement to balance their budgets, they cut welfare benefits. The final result is that we have carried out a redistribution of income in America in recent decades, from the young to the old.[16]

Finally, both poverty and welfare seem to be becoming more of inherited traits. Increasingly, applicants for welfare were themselves members of welfare families when they were young. In part this is because welfare became more broadly available, especially in poor states, at about the time today's young adults were born. There simply are more adults who were themselves on welfare as children who are now old enough to have children. However, there also seems to be evidence that those who were poor for long periods of time when they were children, especially if they lived in areas where a lot of other poor people lived, are likely to become poor adults.[17]

These trends are an indictment of contemporary American society and a challenge to our beliefs about ourselves. In a nation that prides itself on equal opportunity, the proportion of its population that is poor is growing. In a nation that worships youth and has seen itself as youthful, one in five of its children are poor. In a nation that has always told itself stories of upward mobility—about noble poor individuals who became great successes—poverty seems increasingly to close off people's futures. These trends challenge the very soul of the American myth in our time. Thus, they raise serious questions about our religious sense of who we are and want to be.

FOUR FACTORS THAT LEAD TO POVERTY

Much of the remainder of this book offers detailed analyses of various explanations of trends such as these. At this point I merely want to suggest four factors that various analysts may discuss. We shall return to these four factors at the end of our inquiry to see what we have learned.

First, it is essential to remember that poverty decreases when the economy grows well and increases when the economy slows down. This seems obvious enough but is often forgotten when comparing poverty rates over time. Poverty was relatively low in 1973–74, when the economy was growing pretty well, and relatively high in 1983, at the end of a deep recession. In order to identify underlying trends in the economy, it is necessary to look at poverty rates at comparable points in the business cycle—two recession years or two expansion years.

To make the same point in a different way, poverty declined from 18.5 percent in 1959 to 8.8 percent in 1974. Some of this was due to public policy directly aimed at poverty, but most of it was due to the long period of rapid economic expansion over those years. Similarly, the increase in poverty since 1974 is mostly due to slower economic growth since then. During this same period of time, wages for all Americans have failed to keep pace with inflation.[18] The great American middle class has experienced real economic stress over these years; some have even fallen into poverty. More often this decline in real wages has pushed the near poor under the official poverty standard. As we look to the future, the lesson is clear. The best anti-poverty program America has ever known is a growing economy. That is not likely to change.

Second, what has changed and seems likely to continue doing so is what kind of jobs the economy needs to have performed.[19] It is often described as a shift from a manufacturing to a service economy, but that does not fully describe the nature of the changes. Well-paying blue-collar jobs, most of them unionized, have been and are disappearing. Most of these jobs did not require much formal education, although any of us who tried working them (if only briefly) can testify that they did take skill. Most of the boys I went to high school with in East Moline, Illinois, went directly from high school to a well-paying job in the farm implement industry under a United Auto Workers contract, and those jobs made them middle class. Their children cannot do the same because those jobs are not available. If their children go to college or technical school, they may do even better than their parents, making more money with less physical labor. If, however, those children do not finish high school or only do so, they are likely to end up as a nurse's aide or as a laborer in a non-union manufacturing company being paid wages low enough to compete with foreign wages.

The result is a number of trends in income distribution leading in various directions. Well-educated workers, many of them younger, are moving up in income. Indeed, one major shift in income in recent years is an increase in the number of relatively well-off Americans. At the same time many Americans, many of them middle aged, have fallen from the middle class as their well-paying jobs disappeared. Particularly difficult is the situation of middle-aged, formerly well-paid factory workers without much formal education whose jobs disappear. It is easier to say that they should retrain themselves than to do it. Finally, those without much formal education, who never got into a well-paying manufacturing job, are not likely to become middle class. At the very center of all of these labor market trends is formal education, which more than ever decides economic success.

This brings us to the third factor. There is considerable evidence that American society is becoming increasingly divided physically by income. William Julius Wilson, whose analysis we shall consider in greater detail later, is the best-known advocate of this view.[20] However, poverty experts from across the political spectrum have described the same phenomenon in different ways. It is seen most clearly in our contemporary American metropolitan landscape. Our cities have always had neighborhoods where a lot of poor people lived. In the past these same cities were also centers of economic growth and job expansion. That is no longer the case. Increasingly, jobs are expanding in the suburban ring of most of our cities and declining within the cities.

More and more, cities are seen as the place where people live who cannot afford to get out to the suburbs. True or not, city neighborhoods are considered dirty, unfriendly, and unsafe. Certainly crack cocaine has reinforced this impression with its attendant images of violence and disorder.

The city is probably not as bad and the suburbs not as good a place to live as people believe. The objective truth is irrelevant, as long as people believe and act on those beliefs. There seems to be considerable evidence that those of middle income have fled city neighborhoods, leaving them to the poor. The result is neighborhoods where role models of working adults and connections to jobs decline along with community institutions. One key example of what we have already discussed is schools. Some schools serve primarily poor children, others serve primarily middle-income students, and still others serve primarily affluent students. Under these conditions, equal educational opportunity would be possible only if much more money were spent on the children in the schools serving the poor who show up at school with considerable educational handicaps. Instead, educational funding in America is largely local, meaning schools serving affluent kids typically spend more per pupil than those serving poor ones.

If, in fact, education is increasingly what decides our long-term economic success, then unequal educational opportunity makes inherited poverty even more likely. We like to tell ourselves stories of young people who grow up in poor neighborhoods and go to their schools and yet succeed against these odds. Once again, our actions speak louder than our words. Few of those who repeat these stories of heroic success choose to send their own children to schools in low-income neighborhoods. Perhaps we could overcome this inequality in education through massive subsidies to schools serving low-income students. Can anyone seriously imagine suburban voters agreeing to have their taxes used for this purpose? Would they prefer instead to have their neighborhoods and schools integrated by income and race? Sooner or later any serious attempt to deal with poverty will have to face these realities of our social division.

This leads us to the fourth factor, public policy. While public policy can support or handicap economic growth, especially long term, politicians seem as much victims as masters of the business cycle. For generations, economists have argued at length over just how much

21

political decisions can shape the market. All but a few agree that political decisions can help or hurt economic growth to some extent. Similarly, government policy may have been able to retard the decline of high-paying manufacturing jobs. It certainly can do more or less in helping workers cope with these changes. Finally, suburbs were built with a lot of government help for highways and water and sewer systems and for VA or FHA loans for housing. In other words, we should not forget that all of these first three factors have significant public policy dimensions. However, there is a fourth factor of some considerable significance: public policy aimed directly at the distribution of income in the United States.

Once again, we shall consider these matters in considerable detail later. Here it is enough to note that the past two decades have seen some significant cuts in domestic social programs that served those with lower incomes.[21] At the same time, taxes were cut for people with higher incomes. These changes reinforced some of the trends already mentioned, increasing the gap between the rich and the poor in the eighties. Those hurt most were the working poor and near poor, some of whom were pushed below the official poverty level. Welfare benefits also did not keep pace with cost-of-living increases during these years. At the same time, programs such as day care and job training, which were designed to help people escape poverty, were cut. Welfare policy itself was changed in ways that made it cost more to go to work. It should not be surprising that these policy changes alone led to an increase in poverty.

One thesis of this book is that everything is related to everything else. All four of the factors just mentioned reinforce one another.[22] A slow economy not only directly produces more poverty; it also speeds up the decline in well-paying blue-collar jobs, exacerbates the deterioration of city neighborhoods, and produces budget pressure on direct government assistance. Similarly, a negative turn in any of the other factors will create problems for the other three. Happily, an improvement in any of the four will also lead to improvement in the other three. The lesson to be learned is that there is no single simple solution to problems as complex as poverty, but that improvements of any sort have positive effects on other factors. One final conclusion may be obvious. Any attempt to reverse the trends in poverty—its recent growth, the younger age of those in it, and its transmission from generation to generation—must take into account a variety of factors. If the four I have suggested are not enough or not the right ones, then we must identify other factors. In any event, I doubt any single factor will tell the whole story or guide an adequate response to this issue of poverty in United States.

THE STRUCTURE OF THIS BOOK

In the following eleven chapters, we shall try to come to terms with this issue of poverty in our common life. First, we will review the history of poverty as a public issue in the United States and then the history of welfare policy. We shall then present four distinctively different contemporary analyses of poverty and welfare—those of Charles Murray, Lisbeth Schorr, Lawrence Mead, and Frances Fox Piven. In each case we shall attempt to identify the key ethical assumptions driving the analysis. Then, we shall reflect upon the religious meaning of these ethical assumptions and develop a view of human life that provides critical distance from them. Based upon this theological position we shall return to the topics of poverty and welfare with a new perspective and then propose policy for the future. Throughout, we want always to remember that the real question at stake is what sort of world would promise a meaningful future for Shawn and Marie. We have our work cut out for us.

CHAPTER TWO

NOTHING NEW:
THE HISTORY OF POVERTY AS A PUBLIC
ISSUE IN THE UNITED STATES

T hree times in this century poverty has become a significant public issue in the United States. These times are usually called the Progressive Era, the New Deal, and the Great Society. This is not to say that poverty did not exist or that people did not know about it before 1900. They did. However, they typically considered it the personal problem of the poor, not a public issue for all of us. It was not until industrialization and urbanization joined together to produce both great wealth and mass urban poverty that the gap between rich and poor could not be ignored. At the same time, the developing interest in social science provided the tools to begin to measure the extent and causes of mass urban poverty amid general prosperity. These new realities and new insights led many to conclude that poverty was a public issue. Each of the three times that the concern about poverty and efforts to do something about it received significant support, war intervened and a desire to return to normalcy followed. In the United States, normalcy has always meant ignoring poverty as a public issue. Yet poverty remains, and many of us continue to see it as a central issue in American life. As we try to think about poverty as a public issue we have much to learn from those who have sought to do the same in the past.

BEFORE THE TWENTIETH CENTURY

The roots of the pre–twentieth-century attitudes and practices toward poverty have been summarized in these terms: "The Puritans of the Massachusetts Bay Colony brought with them the theology of Calvin, the social attitudes of the English middle classes and the welfare machinery of Queen Elizabeth."[1] The Elizabethan poor law was marked by localism and severity. Each parish was responsible for the support of its own poor. Those unable to work might be supported in their homes; those able to work had to accept work, including that provided by almshouses or by contract with local employers, or go to jail. While colonial America offered unbounded opportunity for work, it also offered a very good chance of being relatively poor. At least most other people were also poor, and for most that poverty was not as bad as it had been in Europe.[2] Certainly there was plenty of work around for people to do, and most were struggling hard just to survive. Given these economic realities, it should not be surprising that the colonists expressed little sympathy for those who were poor unless it was clearly a case of misfortune. Yet records suggest the poor could expect considerable help from family, neighbors, and limited private charity (primarily from churches). Especially those considered unable to work also could hope to receive some support from local government in pre–Civil War America.[3] By official doctrine, both religious and secular, poverty signified a personal or moral flaw in the poor individual and thus had to be discouraged by harsh and uncompromising penalties. In practice this doctrine often was tempered by simple human concern.

Of the options available at the time, the almshouse emerged as the preferred method for care of the poor in nineteenth-century America. It was not thought as open to corruption and abuse as either of the other accepted alternatives—contracting with employers or auctioning off the poor to those offering to care for them at the lowest price. On the other hand, the almshouse carried the stigma thought necessary to prevent dependency much better than the fourth alternative, direct financial support in the home. Almshouses of this period usually included the dependent of all sorts—the young, the old, the sick, the disabled, the mentally retarded, and the mentally ill. Yet, it was felt that the mere experience of work coupled with the misery of the almshouse would build character and scare away any residual laziness. Despite this stated preference for almshouses in principle, in fact direct financial support (often called outdoor relief) remained by default the primary method of caring for the poor, because almshouses were so difficult to set up and administer and proved inadequate whenever economic depression occurred.

Scientific Charity

By the last quarter of the nineteenth century, science had become popular enough that attempts were made to administer charity scientifically. The central institution of this movement was the Charity Organization Society (COS).[4] Founded in Buffalo in 1877, by 1892 there was a COS in 92 communities, including most of the major American cities. They enlisted community leaders and groups in an effort to systematize and minimize relief. The COS doctrine concerning the causes and preferred treatment for poverty was not new, only applied more consistently. The COS opposed public relief except in the form of institutions (almshouses), which were to serve as a sort of ultimate punishment. This led them into immediate conflict with the State Boards of Charities, whose major accomplishment had been to restrict the catch-all character of almshouses by establishing separate institutions for various forms of dependency such as mental illness and physical handicap. In the long run, the COS theory became dominant, leading to a reduction in direct public relief. Free charity was discouraged except on a systematic basis, including a personal interview by a visitor, who was to lace support liberally with spiritual instruction. In practice this moral toughness was worn down by the reality of need and the lack of volunteers until the COS itself became more and more a relief-granting institution. Over a period of time, the opposition of COS to public assistance evolved into the demand that public assistance adopt the scientific methods COS had developed. And so the COS visitor evolved into the welfare caseworker.[5]

Although the full impact of industrialization and urbanization was not felt until near the turn of the century, the tremors could be detected much earlier. During the pre–Civil War depression of 1857–1858, the poor organized themselves for the first time to demand increased public works.[6] By 1873, a depression that could be considered industrial in nature was accompanied by agitation by the Knights of Labor.[7] A series of deep industrial depressions in the 1890s, coupled with the general absence of public relief, strained private charity to the breaking point. After the Civil War, great numbers of immigrants arrived in the United States destined not to plant farms

27

on the frontier but to work in the factories and to live in the slums of cities. By the end of the nineteenth century, the United States was faced with an urban scene in which the expected poverty of personal misfortune was surrounded by marginal employment at low wages and, from time to time, by massive industrial unemployment. Based on an amalgam of the puritanism of the colonists and the social Darwinism of the gilded age of industrialization, the generally held understanding of poverty was that it was the fate suffered by those who lacked the moral character or individual initiative to succeed. This was simply increasingly less persuasive in explaining the facts of the time.

POVERTY DISCOVERED—THE PROGRESSIVE ERA

If any individual is to be credited with the discovery of poverty as a public issue in the United States, it would be Robert Hunter, whose book simply entitled *Poverty* was published in 1904.[8] In that book, Hunter advanced three novel propositions. First, he distinguished between dependency (receiving private or public assistance) and the much broader category of poverty. Second, he contended that poverty was much more widespread than generally supposed at the time— specifically that, if a family income of $460 per year was taken as the poverty standard, over ten million Americans were poor (20 percent of the population in the industrial states and 10 percent in the agricultural ones).[9] Finally, he concluded that, since the vast majority of the poor—as opposed to the dependent—were poor because of social forces, not personal weakness, changes in the social system were needed to deal with poverty. Hunter summarized his position this way:

> There is unquestionably a poverty which men deserve. But as surely as this is true, there is also the poor which we must not always have with us. The poor of this latter class are, it seems to me, the mass of the poor; they are bred of miserable and unjust social conditions which punish the good and the pure, the faithful and industrious, the slothful and the vicious all alike . . . and the wrongful action of such social and economic forces is a preventable thing.[10]

These remained the hallmarks of the pre–World War I reformers: poverty included many more than just those who sought charity; it was widespread, and would require social and political change.

Settlement Houses

While Hunter deserves great credit for his work, it might well be argued that poverty was discovered as a public issue not by any one person but rather by a form of association—the settlement house. Upon graduation from Indiana University in 1896, Robert Hunter became the organizing secretary of the Chicago Board of Charities and in time moved into Hull House. He left Chicago in 1902 to become the head worker at the University Settlement House in New York. His experience is of a piece with a number of his contemporaries, middle-class young people who took up residence amid the urban poor. In many ways, these settlement houses were quite typically middle class, yet they formed the core of social reform for years to come. Their importance was not marked, especially at first, by the quality of their programs but rather by a thirst for open inquiry and a drive for action.

To say that the settlement-house workers were typically middle class is to imply that they were in continuity with the COS visitors, and this is accurate to an extent. Both the settlement-house workers and the COS visitors were critical of dependency and adamantly in favor of self-help over indiscriminate almsgiving. Both considered personal relationships between the poor and nonpoor vital. While the COS visitors sought such relations in order to instruct the poor, the settlement-house workers wanted to learn from the poor in turn. But perhaps the most critical common element of both was their commitment to scientific inquiry. As the COS visitors went about the task of identifying the causes of pauperism scientifically, they began to discover that there were social as well as personal causes.[11] By picking up these findings and extending their own research but a few steps further, the settlement-house workers began identifying some of these social causes, emphasizing their importance, and proposing action to deal with them. These may have been a few steps from the theory, and especially from the mature practice of the COS, but they were quite critical steps indeed. They led to the settlements' concern for political action rather than the private philanthropy of the COS. Apparently what tipped the balance was the recognition that the settlement-house workers gained through associating with the poor as equals. The settlement-house workers saw that what distinguished the rich from the poor was not personal character so much as social situation.[12] Thus a group of typical middle-class young people came to the urban scene with a rather simplistic desire to be of service to those in need. Because their minds were open to the people and events around them, they were forged into what may well have been the most vital force ever in American social reform.

Neighbors and Democrats

What was the character of the settlement houses that led to such dramatic changes in persons' lives?[13] The most obvious difference from previous approaches to poverty was that the settlement house was located within the community of the poor. The COS visitor considered it his or her responsibility to show the poor how the other half lived as an incentive to them for seek to rise above their poverty; the settlement-house worker identified himself or herself as a part of the poor neighborhood. While initially a matter of geography, this difference pointed to much more. Settlement houses attempted in the first instance to provide services that the neighborhood needed. The results were visiting nurses, day care, English language classes, boys and girls clubs, after-school classes for youth, evening classes for parents, and job counseling. In those cases where needed services were properly the responsibility of public bodies, the settlement houses joined or led their neighbors in trying to get them. These efforts were aimed at everything from sewage and garbage disposal and police and fire protection to parks and educational services and separate juvenile courts. The settlements were first and foremost a part of the community; they sought brotherhood and justice, not charity.

This neighborliness laid the ground work for the other central characteristic of the settlement house movement—a consistent commitment to democratic politics. This commitment was manifested in two ways. First, the internal process and principles used in settlement houses were intended to be democratic. Unlike the COS, for whom the poor had not yet earned the right of citizenship, the settlement house assumed the poor had opinions that mattered as much as those of the wealthy. Thus, the life of the settlements was marked by forums and similar procedures by which such opinions could be shared, common purposes developed, and common action undertaken. In addition, many of the other programs of the settlement, such as

language classes, were designed to undergird this democratic participation. Obviously, these political processes both assumed and extended the neighborliness already discussed. Both are finally based
on a mutuality shared by those who recognize one another as equals.

The second way in which this commitment to democratic politics
manifested itself was in the continual insistence that the social problems faced by the urban poor were in fact political issues for a
democratic society. Armed with statistics, settlement house workers
and their constituents proceeded to make their case for reform to
government officials. This shift from social problem to political issue
once again assumed the equality of rich and poor. On the basis of
their association with the poor, the settlement house workers were
prepared to make just that claim. Thus the settlement worker's
commitment to democratic politics not only influenced their style of
association but also pushed them toward political action. One institution, the settlement house, brought together identification with the
everyday problems of the poor and a commitment to the alleviation
of those problems democratically.

The Progressives

Just as Robert Hunter was a representative of this particular form
of association, the development of settlement houses was but one
crucial aspect of a more general cultural shift.[14] Americans had always
been opposed to poverty, seeing their country as the place where
everyone had the opportunity to escape poverty if he or she tried. Yet,
as has been suggested, most Americans remained near poverty. In the
late nineteenth century a social paradox developed. Because of the
vast development of industry, great wealth had been generated, giving
rise to the hope that perhaps poverty was not the inevitable fate of
most of humanity. This increase in wealth was publicly documented,
along with accounts of both the ruthless and sometimes fraudulent
manner in which the fortunes had been accumulated and the scan-
dalous ways in which they were being expended. At the same time,
periodic severe depression swept the land, bringing not only additional misery to those already poor but also poverty to broader
numbers. The contradiction of persistent poverty amid the newly
established wealth was not lost upon the public at large and, particularly, upon social reformers. While there were no apparent reasons

why poverty should continue, social inquiry did begin to document factors other than personal character upon which it seemed to feed. The paradoxical persistence of poverty amid economic growth and the new explorations of the social causes of poverty led to the old moralisms being replaced by the broader definitions of poverty proposed by people like Robert Hunter.

This is not to suggest that the settlements' understanding of poverty became a majority opinion or even that their proposals for action were well received. Rather, legislation and institutional change came very slowly, if at all. Since the reformers shared in the traditional aversion to pauperism, they did not generally attempt direct changes in the poor law. Instead, they sought protection for workers and compensation for those groups of persons who ought not be expected to work. They also worked for reforms in other areas important to poor neighborhoods such as housing and education. One after another, voluntary associations were generated from the settlement houses themselves—associations that developed the rationale, the data, and the strategy to be used in the legislative battles to come. These legislative battles usually included hearings at which reformers appeared, armed with massive doses of data and personal accounts from those affected, coupled with coverage by the progressive press and personal reminders to the legislators who wavered. Most of these efforts focused on the local and state level, partially because most previous attempts at national social legislation had been ruled unconstitutional. Locally, the results included regulatory laws on such things as tenements, as well as direct reforms in educational, health, welfare, and criminal justice institutions. The legislative results on the state level included workmen's compensation, child labor and women's hours laws, and minimum wages, as well as meager public assistance for the blind, aged, and mothers.[15] On the national level, only workmen's compensation and child labor laws were passed. Most of the energy went into passing and attempting to enforce antitrust laws. As a whole, all of this legislation fell far short of the goals sought by reformers both in terms of coverage and in terms of adequacy of benefits. Fuller enactment awaited a later time.

As I have suggested, most of these legislative efforts had a solid foundation in the associational life of the settlement houses. Therefore, these efforts were based upon exposure to the concrete realities of poverty and an experience of debate and action that had established common purposes. However, the general public had fastened its attention on the sensational accounts of governmental and industrial corruption and centralization. As a result the broader movement, generally referred to as Progressivism, had much less of a commitment to a comprehensive program of social reform than to a more limited program of governmental and anti-monopolistic reform. The Progressives centered their attack on breaking up city machine governments and industrial monopolies. These efforts were based much more on the presumed virtues of atomized middle-class individualism than on any associational experience, such as that of the settlement houses. It was this watered-down form of reform that prevailed, in the persons of Theodore Roosevelt and Woodrow Wilson, and collapsed in the face of World War I.

There is a certain ambiguity in the historical judgments about the status of reform in the postwar decade.[16] It does appear clear that the nation came out of the war drained of energy and yearning for normalcy. Concretely, this led to the Red scare and a more general pulling back from prewar social reforms through legislative repeals and judicial rulings. Certainly no new social measures were enacted, unless one includes Prohibition (itself a symptom of the return to private moralism). At the same time, social-work professionals became interested in psychological explanations of human behavior, leading most of the new recruits into the profession away from social reform and toward personal adjustment.[17] Clearly Progressivism, broadly understood, died in the war, but to say that reform died is to confuse Progressivism with the reform efforts that had emerged from the experience of the settlements. Beneath the surface of normalcy, many of the individual reformers and voluntary associations that had arisen out of the settlements, as well as the settlements themselves, continued their work. That work was lonely at times and results were sparse, but the groundwork was laid during this period for most of the enduring social policy of the New Deal.[18]

THE DISCOVERY OF UNEMPLOYMENT—THE NEW DEAL

Whatever problems the early reformers may have had communicating the importance of poverty amid the general economic growth of the early decades of the twentieth century were not shared by the reformers of the 1930s. Americans did not really discover unemployment; they fell victim to it. In the face of the Great Depression, unemployment became a public issue out of sheer necessity. That action followed is uncontestable! Whether that action displayed any consistent character, and what that character might have been, remain matters of some controversy. Some marks of the New Deal that distinguish it from earlier reform follow from the reality of the Great Depression. It was not confined to a minority. Whereas most Americans believed they were either middle class or could become so during the Progressive Era, most Americans were afraid they were soon to be poor in the Great Depression. Not only was the economic system not working well for a residual group, it did not seem to be working too well for anyone. Those politicians, such as Hoover, who argued at first that the Depression was a state and local problem, were not persuasive for long. It was clearly national. The story of the New Deal must be told in terms of federal legislation and administration. Finally, it was massive. Certainly a few of the more visionary of the earlier reformers had drawn the broadest possible implications about the action required, but in the depths of the Depression nearly everyone agreed that something major had to be done.

Franklin Roosevelt took office in 1932 with a clear promise to do something and with apparent uncertainty as to just what to do. The result was the New Deal, but that term covers far too much to be discussed in general. Historians have usually distinguished between two phases of the New Deal, the former typified by National Recovery Administration (NRA) controls and the latter by Keynesian fiscal policy. The NRA was but a slight modification of proposals advanced by businessmen for the purpose of stabilizing prices (i.e., holding them up) by allowing the appropriate industries to set price standards and, in cooperation with the labor unions, wage standards. In 1935, buoyed by Democrat congressional victories and concerned about populist criticisms of his early programs, Roosevelt turned to increased government spending to stimulate the economy using as a theoretical justification the Keynesian emphasis on demand stimulation.

The difference between the NRA and Keynesian fiscal policy probably cannot be overemphasized. Indeed, the discovery of the role of government expenditure as an economic stimulus is a major discovery of the New Deal, although it was not fully practiced until the war began, and then unintentionally. Yet, both the NRA and Keynesian fiscal policy had economic recovery as their major goal, with only the subsidiary aim of dealing with poverty. Running through both phases of the New Deal, although with greater emphasis in the latter phase, were specific attempts to deal with poverty through direct relief, social insurance, and wage and hours standards. It is these efforts that mark the second occasion in this century when there was action aimed specifically at reducing poverty.

Harry Hopkins

If Robert Hunter represented the reform movement's understanding of poverty during the Progressive Era, Harry Hopkins did so for the New Deal.[19] As the chief administrator of the Federal Emergency Recovery Administration (FERA), the Civil Works Administration (CWA), and the Works Progress Administration (WPA), Hopkins probably had more influence on New Deal policy affecting the poor than any other person. Directly out of Grinnell College in Iowa, Hopkins was introduced to urban poverty when he took a job as a settlement-house worker in New York City in 1912. He became a prominent administrator of private welfare in that city, became the administrator of New York State emergency relief for Governor Roosevelt after 1929, and then migrated to Washington in 1933 to head FERA.

Hopkins held two central tenets. The first, a result of his background as a social worker, was that the dignity of the poor and unemployed should be respected and supported. In general, this led Hopkins to seek levels of support high enough to provide proper housing, clothing, and medical care, as well as food, and to prefer work relief over direct financial support where possible and monetary relief over food vouchers or commodities where necessary. As a result, Hopkins frowned upon intricate determinations of eligibility as demeaning and encouraged diversified work projects so workers could retain and develop skills. Hopkins' second central tenet was that government had a responsibility to the poor and the unemployed. This was an extension of principles articulated by Roosevelt himself, but Hopkins stated them much more concretely than Roosevelt, becoming a sort of permanent lobby for the poor within the New Deal.

In practice Hopkins merged these two tenets, as seen in a campaign speech in 1936:

> I don't believe ever again in America are we going to permit the things to happen that have happened in the past to people. . . . We are coming to the day when we are going to have decent houses for the poor, when there is genuine and real security for everybody. I have gone all over the moral hurdles that people are poor because they are bad. I don't believe it. A system of government on that basis is fallacious.[20]

Federal Bureaucrats

Hopkins represents a vast reawakening to the plight of the poor. Most of this reawakening was located outside of government, and much of it was quite critical of the New Deal. Yet in a more direct way, Hopkins represents the major new organizational setting for this reawakened interest in the poor—the federal bureaucracy.[21] Many of the bureaucrats who shared Hopkins' interest in the poor also shared, in one way or another, his experience in settlement houses and private welfare agencies. However, as the bureaucracies expanded and matured they developed a structure of their own. In time, this structure led the bureaucrats to see the poor not as neighbors but as clients. This did not erase either the general respect or particular pragmatic commitments that had developed because of previous experience, such as a continual concern for the dignity and independence of the poor and commitments to work relief, social insurance, and wage and hours standards. It did sever those contacts that would have provided continual checks upon policy formulation. Instead of being leaders or representatives of poor communities, the bureaucrats became spokesmen and champions for the cause of the poor.

If democratic politics provided the integrating factor in the life of the settlement house, it was also the guiding rationale of the New Deal. Above all else, the New Deal stressed that in a democracy the government must be responsive to the needs of its citizens. However, the federal bureaucracy required the efficiency of hierarchical structure at least as much as the creative dialogue of democratic politics. In any event, the poor themselves were not participants in whatever internal dialogue occurred. Bureaucrats did not represent the poor; they served the interests of the poor. But in the crush of national politics and planning, the interests of the poor quite easily became one set of interests among a whole variety of interests. The New Deal tried to serve all of these interests or at least those that seemed most important, without any clear way of evaluating any of them.

If my discussion of the New Deal bureaucracy as a base for considering the issue of poverty seems unduly harsh, it is not meant to be. Some of the most visionary of the Progressives only dreamed of major action by the federal government to alleviate poverty; New Deal bureaucrats actually tried to accomplish this. These efforts should not be underestimated. In retrospect, the federal bureaucracy displayed certain weaknesses as a base for reform because it tended to turn citizens into clients and democratic politics into interest-group bargaining. On the other hand, it must also be admitted that the negative character of these tendencies was less apparent in the Depression era, when such vast numbers of people sought help and the unemployed constituted such a large pressure group. In more "normal" times and contexts when there are relatively fewer of the poor, these tendencies may lead to a minority of the population being subject to the indignities of the client status and the hopelessness of an insignificant interest group.

The New Deal

Certainly many of the weaknesses that developed in the second era of reform in the twentieth century are related to its location within the New Deal. The central problem addressed by the New Deal was not the elimination of poverty but general economic recovery. This commitment to economic growth was not new. What was new was the assumption, as much a result of Hoover's failures as of different intellectual positions, that the federal government must play an active role in accomplishing economic stability. Given a reluctance to bypass private industry in this process, the character of the federal government's role was never clear. What was clear is that the New Deal programs were geared to restoring confidence in the economic system, not to changing it radically. For this reason, New Deal reforms were essentially oriented toward the middle class, protecting the interests of the vast majority of the citizens.

Those advocating programs specifically aimed at eliminating poverty were required to make a case for the role of such programs within the overriding concern of general economic recovery. Whenever such programs seemed to endanger this overriding concern, either by retarding economic recovery or by alienating powerful groups within the coalition supporting economic recovery, they were in real peril. So these programs were constantly subject to legislative compromise and administrative pressure dictated by concerns other than the elimination of poverty. In summary, it is fair to say that the New Deal neither reorganized the economy nor significantly redistributed wealth.[22] Rather, it provided a minimal level of security for private enterprise, and to a lesser extent for individuals, in order to preserve capitalism.[23]

There was nothing very startling in the social legislation arising during the New Deal, except that it was national in scope. Temporary work relief had become a tradition at the local level. Now it became a national program handicapped in planning by its temporary nature and eliminated when the war solved the unemployment problem. As we have seen, pension and direct assistance for the unemployed, aged, handicapped, and mothers had been instituted in many states before 1935.[24] Now it became national Social Security, which included both compulsory social insurance primarily for retirement benefits and categorical aid programs with methods for determining need, which must have been quite familiar to veterans of the COS. Wage and hour standards had been common elements in the Progressive reform programs. Now such standards became federal law. In a sense these elements of the New Deal brought to fruition the program of the earlier reformers, which had been refined and kept alive by various volunteer groups during the 1920s.[25] However, the requirements of the Roosevelt coalition led to some severe restrictions, both in terms of coverage and in terms of level of benefit or wage standard. Yet before we completely denigrate these laws, we should note that they remain the general structure of social policy in the United States today.

Normalcy Again

Once again the inability to extend the basis of reform beyond a limited constituency spelled the doom of the commitment to end poverty. When war again entered the picture, it not only diverted attention but provided the ultimate stimulus for the economy. Economic recovery resulted, eliminating the only broadly held rationale for aid of the poor—widespread unemployment. Perhaps this shift is best symbolized by Harry Hopkins himself, who left the relief agencies to become one of Roosevelt's chief foreign policy aides during the war.

With the end of the war, the desire for a return to normalcy dominated American life once more. The remnants of the New Deal remained in at least two senses. The first may be seen in the Full Employment Act of 1946. In rhetoric, the act sets as a goal the provision of employment opportunity for all Americans seeking work; in this sense it can be seen as filling out the New Deal package of social legislation. In fact it is an institutionalization of the government's role in fostering stable economic growth and, as such, formalizes the major element in the New Deal. The second sense in which the New Deal lived on after the war was in the staffs of the various government bureaucracies dealing with the poor. Although the weaknesses in the relationship between bureaucrat and client as a basis for social policy became increasingly apparent, groups and individuals remained within the bureaucracies (and their fellow travelers among the academics) who were as knowledgeable about the nature of poverty and as committed to its elimination as any group other than the poor themselves. In the new context, they simply lacked much of the capacity to act that they had possessed during the New Deal. So the major social legislation passed under Truman was limited to the Housing Act of 1949; national health insurance, federal aid to education, and civil rights legislation were proposed but failed. Under Eisenhower nothing of consequence was added.

THE REDISCOVERY OF POVERTY—THE GREAT SOCIETY

On March 16, 1964, Lyndon Johnson sent a message to Congress outlining the proposed War on Poverty, which concluded with these stirring words:

> On similar occasions in the past we have often been called upon to wage war against foreign enemies which have threatened our freedom. Today we are asked to declare war on a domestic enemy which threatens the strength of our nation and the welfare of our people.[26]

It must be admitted that at the time, the enemy was unknown to the American public at large. More like the Progressive Era than the New Deal, 1964 was a time of relative economic well-being. Not only were most Americans not poor, but they also assumed very few others were, except by choice. The impetus for action did not arise from the majority, as in the case of the New Deal; neither in any direct sense did it arise from community institutions as it had in the Progressive Era. Rather the War on Poverty was invented by professional reformers in response to some very particular problems.[27]

This is not to suggest that the War on Poverty did not have its antecedents on both the local and national levels. On the local level, the context was set by the public appearance of civil rights organizations (especially as the civil rights movement began to turn to the northern cities), a resurgence of community organizations (influenced to a great degree by the work of Saul Alinsky), and the growing recognition of urban decay (with the resulting cries from city governments for help). The immediate occasion for the analysis and strategy that informed the later national effort was the failure of urban renewal.[28] By the early 1960s it was clear that urban renewal often brought new buildings, new enterprises, and new people, but it seldom solved old problems. Urban renewal was supposed to eliminate slums. Instead it either moved them, by displacing the poor into new areas, or concentrated them by putting the poor together in large public housing complexes. In any event, the social character of the slum remained—poor education, poor health, high crime rate, high unemployment, and high welfare costs.

In a quite different context, a public discussion of poverty had been developing for some time. As early as 1958, John Kenneth Galbraith had contrasted America's private wealth with its public squalor, although he had suggested that poverty had been reduced to a regional and personal issue.[29] Henry Caudill had documented the depth of the problem for one particular region, Appalachia.[30] Contrary to Galbraith, Gabriel Kolko argued that mass poverty remained and that income distribution was in fact becoming less equal.[31] By 1962, Robert Lampman had documented statistically the continued existence of mass poverty, although he expected a major portion of it would soon be eliminated by economic growth alone.[32] Michael Harrington described the human misery symbolized in these statistics and added a sense of moral outrage about the existence of this poverty in such a rich land.[33]

However, other pressures were also building.[34] While planning a tax cut to stimulate economic growth, the Council of Economic Advisors started to search for a program of public expenditure for the expected increased tax revenues when that economic growth occurred. At the same time, President Kennedy was in search of a way to respond to the growing civil rights movement that would not be directly abrasive to whites, especially the working class who were poor. Finally, the president was casting about for a domestic program that would set the same sort of moral tone for his administration that the Peace Corps offered on the international front. When Theodore Sorensen (Kennedy's speech writer) introduced the president to an extremely readable review of the literature on poverty by Dwight Macdonald[35] and Walter Heller (Kennedy's top economic advisor) continued to suggest some sort of program of public expenditure for the poor, Kennedy ordered Heller to draw up plans for a war on poverty. When introduced to the idea after Kennedy's assassination, Lyndon Johnson adopted it and soon officially declared war.

Ohlin and Cloward

It is somewhat more difficult to identify particular individuals who are representative of this era of reform. Yet, at the center of those efforts—which were to solidify into the major new program of the period, community action—stood a small number of persons deeply committed to a particular approach to fighting poverty. Lloyd Ohlin and Richard Cloward are excellent examples of this approach. Having both received doctorates from major universities, Ohlin and Cloward were serving together on the faculty of the Columbia University School of Social Work by 1956. Their first major joint effort was a book on juvenile delinquency, *Delinquency and Opportunity*,[36] which presented a particular theory of delinquency. Put simply, Cloward and Ohlin argued that delinquency was primarily caused not by problems with the individuals or the groups to which they belonged but by broader social forces. Specifically, they contended that delinquent youth internalized the values of a success-oriented culture but had no means of realizing those values and so in frustration turned to delinquency instead. This theory stood in stark contrast not only to the individualistic emphasis of the majority of social workers who were greatly influenced by psychology but also to the theory that delinquent gangs represented subcultures with such different values that their members did not have the same sense of right and wrong as the rest of us.

In the long run, however, its major attraction to activists was not its theory but the practical implications flowing from it. Cloward and Ohlin state these implications in this way:

> The target for preventive action, then, should be defined, not as the individual or group that exhibits the delinquent pattern, but as the social setting that gives rise to delinquency. It is our view, in other words, that the major effort of those who wish to eliminate delinquency should be directed to the reorganization of slum communities.[37]

This theory was appealing not only because it was new, but also because it fit in quite neatly with the concerns of a number of those seeking to deal with urban problems politically.

Mobilization for Youth

While the particular contribution of Cloward and Ohlin should be kept in mind, they illustrate a much broader movement. First of all, a large number of other faculty members and students from Columbia were deeply involved in Mobilization for Youth, a project in Harlem that tried to put into practice the theory of delinquency and social change in Cloward and Ohlin's book. Moreover, social scientists and planners from universities in other major cities were beginning to play similar activist roles. These experts also staffed the administrations and advisor boards of major private programs such as that of the Ford Foundation. Finally, a number of such experts followed the course of Lloyd Ohlin, who became a consultant and eventually a prime administrator for government programs. Cloward and Ohlin were a part of a major shift in social reform in America. Many of the earlier reformers had been college graduates, but these new reformers were professionals who had received specific training in social work and social planning. Reform was now much too important and sophisticated to be left to amateurs.[38]

Perhaps the character of this reform movement can be seen best by considering Mobilization for Youth and then relating it to some of the other aspects of the broader movement. As we have seen, Cloward and Ohlin were committed to a complete reorganization of the slum community. Two specific implications for Mobilization for Youth flow from theory. First, action was aimed at social, not individual, change. While the funding sources preferred individual counseling, Mobilization for Youth stressed programs in education, employment, legal services, and community organization. Second, as a part of their theory of general institutional failure, Cloward and Ohlin argued that the established institutions (schools, hospitals, government, and political organizations as well as social welfare agencies) represented their own interests rather than those of the community as a whole. For this reason, Mobilization for Youth sought the establishment of broader, direct community organizations for the purpose of coordinating the efforts of these established institutions. While this was usually justified by appeals to comprehensiveness, coordination, and social planning, the real issue was control by the people living in low-income neighborhoods rather than control by outsiders.[39]

Alongside the concern for comprehensive community organization was a commitment to a political process. This commitment not only was stated openly but took a particular form. It was assumed that people seldom, if ever, act out of anything but self-interest. For example, politicians could not be expected to help solve the problems of urban slums unless they felt they had something to gain from such action.[40] Therefore, the community had to develop means of rewarding and punishing public officials if its interests were to be served. Community organization was perceived as the means of forcing not only public officials but other established institutions to meet the needs of the community.[41] Moreover, given the original estimate of human motivation, this community organization itself could proceed only by responding to the self-interest of the individuals and groups in the community. Since Mobilization for Youth assumed there was conflict of interest between the community and other groups and institutions, political conflict could be expected from community organization.

Mobilization for Youth merged a social theory about the causes of delinquency with a political theory about the motivation of human action. The social theory appealed to institutions in search of new approaches and especially to planners looking for something that explained the problems of the urban slum. Policy makers liked it

43

because it called for social changes that political action could apparently bring about: increased educational and employment opportunities. The political theory was not nearly as well received, either because officials did not understand it or because they did not like it. Actually the theory of self-interest was no problem; most political realists agreed on that. But the assumption of a conflict of interests was unacceptable to both established institutions and public officials, who sought harmony, not conflict. This political theory forced Mobilization for Youth into the ambiguous position of often encouraging community groups to make angry demands upon established institutions and at the same time attempting to provide a cooperative framework within which these institutions could respond to these demands with increased services. It was not easy to sit down and work with people who denounced you last week and might do so again next week.

In time this ambiguity grew more difficult to bear as Mobilization for Youth became increasingly militant.[42] When "maximum feasible participation" became a key phrase in the poverty program, it continued to mean quite different things to different people.[43] In the long run, those poverty groups that followed Mobilization for Youth in interpreting participation in terms of conflict provoked reactions from powerful established institutions, which either eliminated the poverty groups or significantly circumscribed their power.[44]

The War on Poverty

Although President Johnson declared war on poverty, the war plan was tattered and the war effort meager. Other than community action, the War on Poverty was composed primarily of old ideas that had been lying around in the federal bureaucracies, most of them since the New Deal. On the whole, these programs stressed education and training as a means of helping individuals escape poverty. While there was a limited number of programs that intentionally created jobs, a major effort in this regard never materialized either for lack of commitment to the idea or for lack of funds. Thus, the various poverty program agencies, local and national, fell back on education and training as the primary antipoverty strategy. Contrary to the expectations of many that the poor were apathetic captives of a cycle of poverty, applicants overwhelmed most of these programs. It soon became obvious that the problem of poverty struck at a much deeper level of public policy: the availability of employment itself. The primary pragmatic lesson learned in the course of the poverty program was that education and job training are of little long-range consequence in abolishing poverty, unless coupled with full employment.[45]

Although the War on Poverty set the political tone of the time, it was but a small part of the Great Society. In housing, urban development, education, social security, medical care, and civil rights, new national commitments were made and federal programs enacted that almost universally sought to shift government services toward the poor and minorities in the United States. However, the war in Vietnam continued to syphon off both money and energy. At the same time, the strategies of conflict used by some of those in the poverty agencies became identified in the public mind with the violence and disruption in the cities and on the campuses. Once again a general longing for normalcy took over. So a new president (Richard Nixon) was elected, the Great Society was slowed, and the dismantling began. This brings us to the specific debate over welfare policy.

CHAPTER THREE

HOW THE POOR CAME TO GET WELFARE: THE HISTORY OF WELFARE POLICY IN THE UNITED STATES

Welfare is an orphan. Everyone—liberal or conservative, right wing or left wing—wants to reduce poverty; no one will defend the current welfare system. How did we get into a situation of trying to address a universally decried problem using a program that no one likes? Surely part of the reason was a lack of foresight and the irrationalities resulting from political compromise. However, our welfare system is finally indefensibly confused because we ourselves are deeply ambiguous about the morality of poverty and welfare. Put simply, we provide more help through simple administrative procedures to those we believe should not be expected to work, and less through complicated administrative procedures to those we believe could or should work. Our perception of who should work and who should not is the great moral divide of welfare policy. Let us be clear that deserving is not finally an administrative or a political term; it is a moral category.[1]

One additional factor that greatly complicates our welfare system is our federal system of government. We do not have a single welfare system; we have hundreds or even thousands of systems. Some welfare is provided by the federal government, some by state governments, and some by local governments. In many cases, programs are shared by more than one level of government. Once again this confusion is due in part to political compromise and the failure to foresee the future. However, once again it is also rooted in our moral ambiguity. Put simply, assistance to those generally viewed as deserving the assistance tends to be assured by the federal government, while assistance to those who are generally viewed as undeserving tends to be left to state and local governments.

In what follows, I intend to tell a simplified story of the development of our welfare system. The story will be placed in the context of broader reform outlined in the previous chapter. Throughout, I shall attempt to make clear that our moral ambiguities lie at the center of this system that no one likes.

As already stated, the legislative results of the Progressive Era occurred at the state and local level. Those with the most significance for future legislation were workmen's compensation; unemployment insurance; child labor; minimum wages; and limited income support for the blind, aged, disabled, and widowed. The most significant piece of welfare legislation passed under the New Deal, the Social Security Act of 1935, merely federalized many of these state programs. However, in doing so it established the basic structure of the social welfare system in the United States right up to the present.

SOCIAL INSURANCE FOR THE MORALLY ACCEPTABLE

A basic distinction in social welfare policy arises here. The largest program established by the Social Security Act of 1935 was Social Security. Primarily a retirement program, Social Security is usually described as social insurance rather than social welfare. What this means is that it is financed by a tax, designated specifically to support this program, and benefits are paid out not on the basis of need but simply because a person has worked in covered employment for the required amount of time. As a result, most people believe that they are just getting back what they paid in when in fact the vast majority of current recipients receive much more than they ever paid in Social Security taxes. In reality, Social Security is financed by a tax on a group generally considered able to pay, current workers, and is paid to a group generally assumed to need it, primarily the elderly. This sounds like welfare—redistributing income from those able to pay to those in need.

Yet, my father was clear that he was not on welfare when he cashed his Social Security check. In part this was because he had paid into the system in the past, but a welfare recipient who worked in the past and paid income tax could argue the same thing. In the final analysis,

Social Security carries with it no social stigma because we believe the elderly deserve it. They worked all of their lives, and the least they can expect is a little support in their retirement. Thus, other groups we consider deserving, elderly spouses and underage surviving children, are included under Social Security. In time other benefits, particularly health care, were added as social insurance. Finally, notice that from the beginning these social insurance programs have been fully funded at the federal level. In sum, we tend to see benefits to those groups we consider most deserving of help as entitlements and to fund them fully even when budgets get tight.[2]

A second social insurance program that was included in the Social Security Act of 1935 was unemployment insurance, designed to assist persons whose jobs disappeared until they were able to find a new job. What the Social Security Act of 1935 did was to leave the administration of these programs at the state level but to provide a federal funding system for these state programs. Morally speaking, most Americans believe that those who lose their jobs through no fault of their own deserve support as long as they are looking for a new one. What must be determined, then, is that the applicant was not at fault for the unemployment and is looking for a job. This is what the federal government left to the states to administer. However, Congress concluded that the involuntarily unemployed deserved federal financing.[3]

CATEGORICAL ASSISTANCE FOR THE MORALLY UNCERTAIN

Little noticed at the time, the Social Security Act of 1935 also included provision of assistance to various categories of people judged deserving of help—the aged, blind, disabled, and single mothers—who were not covered under Social Security. These categorical grants picked up on programs already established in many states during the Progressive Era. The assistance to the aged, blind, and disabled (ABD) came to be called categorical assistance, and the assistance to the children of single mothers came to be called Aid to Dependent Children (ADC). However, neither was totally federalized. Rather, the federal government agreed to pay about half of the cost of these programs, as long as certain federal guidelines were met. However, state and local governments continued to set benefit levels, actually administered the programs, and funded the other half. So it was that the United States did not develop a single welfare program but rather a series of state and local programs all with different benefit levels.

One result of this system is that benefit levels varied widely among states, much more than differences in the local cost of living.[4] The political climate and economic resources of various states and localities led to wide disparities. These programs were also more subject to the budget pressures of state and local governments typically required to balance their budgets each year. This has created periodic crises at the state and local level in bad economic times when government revenue declines at just the time when more people need assistance.[5] Surely, recipients in these categories were treated differently than those falling under Social Security in part because of limited resources at the time. But why did they not find enough money to federalize this program fully also? Once again, I think the answer is one of morality. The people who fall in these categories mostly seem deserving enough but not nearly as clearly as the elderly who have worked and paid into the Social Security system. Some people who are blind, disabled, or mothers work. Why not others? Are persons with psychological problems disabled because they were abused when they were children? Does the mother really not have a man supporting her? Could she work? There is enough ambiguity that these programs had a sort of intermediate moral standing. Their recipients were not judged deserving enough to fall under social insurance but were considered deserving enough to receive significant federal support.

GENERAL ASSISTANCE FOR THE MORALLY SUSPECT

This leaves able-bodied adults who do not have children dependent upon them. Most Americans are not sure such people should get public assistance at all but do not want to see them homeless and hungry. As a result, the federal government has never funded much help for this morally suspect category. However, state and local governments have provided some assistance, typically at lower benefit levels than the other programs and often with stricter administrative procedures. Usually called General Assistance (GA), these programs are often vulnerable to funding cuts when state and local governments run into budget problems.[6]

This general structure established by the Social Security Act of 1935—federal social insurance for the elderly; welfare benefits partially funded by the federal government for low-income people who are elderly, handicapped, or responsible for children; and state and local assistance for able-bodied adults who are very poor—has remained with a few changes up to the present. While this complexity is partially the result of poor planning and political compromise, it is a pretty accurate reflection of the moral views of most Americans. We would like to blame Washington for this often irrational system, but we would do better to look in the mirror. Just who do we think should be expected to support themselves, and who should not? We shall discover that this question is much more complicated than we first think, but the answer is critical to how we structure our social-welfare programs. Moreover, the answer is finally moral.[7]

THE WELFARE SYSTEM EVOLVES

Designed as a residual category as a part of the Social Security Act of 1935, Aid to Dependent Children (ADC) has grown into the program most Americans think of as welfare. It was renamed Aid to Families with Dependent Children (AFDC) along the way to indicate that the adult the children are dependent upon is included in the grant. In 1940, with the United States' economy still in depression, 360,000 families were receiving ADC; by 1960 with the economy in much better shape the number of families on ADC had more than doubled to 745,000.[8] Most Americans and the new president considered this a problem. John F. Kennedy's response was an expanded range of social services, such as day care and job training, intended to move people from welfare to work or to prevent them from needing to go on welfare in the first place.[9]

American farmers are much too productive for their own good. However, they have had enough political influence to protect their interests through various programs that keep prices up, encouraging even more production. One effect is surplus food, much of it owned by the government. One way to get rid of it was simply to give it to public institutions such as schools. So, many of us growing up in the fifties had to eat hash in our school lunchrooms made from surplus food, and some of us even learned to like it. However, government distribution of surplus food was complicated and haphazard, so the solution settled on was food stamps that could be spent at the local grocery store. Shaken by the poverty he saw in West Virginia while running for president, John Kennedy greatly expanded this food stamp program as soon as he took office.[10] It has grown steadily since.

Surely, part of the popularity of food stamps was its benefit to farm states, most of whom did not usually support welfare generously. However, its moral status is not insignificant to its success. Who can deny food to poor people who are mostly elderly, handicapped, or children? Very few, it turns out. However, many can worry about whether the stamps actually get spent on food. So it was that standards were set for what products could not be bought with food stamps. In addition, for years food stamp recipients were required to purchase the full amount of stamps the government said their families needed at a price that varied according to the income of the family. For instance, once a month a family might have been required to pay $100 for $200 worth of stamps. This was intended to assure that the family had enough food to eat even if the rent was not paid. One result was an underground market in food stamps that were sold to pay for other things. It also discouraged participation by those who did not have enough cash to buy a month's supply of food stamps at one time. As a result, this procedure was abandoned in the seventies. In its place appeared an expanded food stamp program that provided them to most recipients free of charge.[11] Throughout, food stamps have always been funded totally by the federal government, in large part because of our moral consensus that even the poor should have enough to eat.[12]

Besides the War on Poverty already discussed, Lyndon Johnson's Great Society brought some other dramatic changes to the welfare system. However, these changes followed old patterns. The most significant new programs were health benefits—Medicare generally for those who qualified for Social Security and Medicaid typically for those who qualified for the categorical programs. As might be expected, Medicare was fully financed and administered by the federal government. Those people considered deserving of Social Security were found equally deserving of Medicare. On the other hand, Medicaid was set up under state or local administration, including the scope of benefits, and was only about half funded by the federal government. The groups who fell within the categories were still considered mostly but not completely deserving.

One other change was designed to address what welfare policy experts call the notch problem. Assuming that it is usually good for those on welfare to go to work at some point, we need to ask what that transition to work will be like. Most welfare recipients cannot step into a well-paying job. The vast majority are mothers with children who require care. They may want the independence that comes with supporting themselves, and they even have dreams of a much better future. However, in many cases it could cost them money to go to work. Jobs that may pay little more than the welfare grant usually involve expenses for such things as transportation, clothes, or food. Why should a mother take a job that will require her to be away from her children and do all of her family work (meals, laundry, cleaning, shopping, etc.) after work, if she will not even be better off economically?

The policy solution for this notch problem is to phase out benefits rather than cut them off totally when a recipient goes to work. So it was that welfare policy was amended in 1967 to enact the thirty-and-a-third rule. That rule said that when a recipient went to work she could keep the first $30 she earned each month without any deduction from her welfare grant. Beyond that first $30, she could then keep one-third of what she made in any month without any deduction from her welfare grant. At a certain income level, depending on family size and state or locality, the welfare grant would end. Let me just note at this point that this amounts to a form of negative income tax (which we will discuss later) limited to those already on welfare. This rule was justified morally on the grounds that it encouraged people to support themselves.[13]

RECENT EFFORTS AT WELFARE REFORM

There is good reason to believe that had Lyndon Johnson been reelected in 1968 he would have sought to pass a welfare reform proposal. He had set up a commission to study the matter, a standard technique for preparing the way for legislative action. Instead, Richard Nixon was elected with the promise to move people from welfare rolls to work rolls. By 1969 the number of families on AFDC had doubled since 1960 to a total of 1,545,000, so there was pressure to act.[14] Heavily influenced by Daniel Patrick Moynihan, Nixon's welfare reform proposal called for additional federal support for the Aid to the Aged, Blind, and Disabled and for a version of a negative income tax to replace Aid to Families with Dependent Children. In time, the AFDC reform failed—that story will be told later. What did happen, however, was that the federal government took over the total cost and administration of the Aid to the Aged, Blind, and Disabled and renamed it Supplemental Security Income (SSI).[15] As a result the aged, blind, and disabled received more generous support less subject to budget cuts and administered in a more tolerant fashion. Once again categories of recipients considered more morally deserving—the aged, blind, and disabled—received better treatment than those seen as more morally suspect—families with poor children.

The other changes instituted by the Nixon administration were designed to eliminate the notch effect in various programs serving the poor. The thirty-and-a-third rule was continued. Food stamps were phased out instead of being cut off abruptly. Residents of subsidized housing were allowed to pay increasing portions of their rent when they made more money rather than having to move out. The heroes at which these changes were targeted were the working poor, those people who remain poor even though they work. Moynihan and George Schultz, then secretary of labor, convinced Nixon that a good conservative Republican should support changes that help the working poor who are trying hard to help themselves.[16] Looming in the background was the question of why people should go to work if they lose all of these benefits and thus are worse off. Both are finally moral, not administrative or political, justifications for these policy changes.

Jimmy Carter proposed welfare reforms roughly like that of Nixon, and they too failed like Nixon's; Ronald Reagan came to Washington pledged to cut domestic spending generally and welfare in particular. In the face of criticism about the human effect of such cuts, Reagan pledged to preserve our safety net for those in need and only cut benefits for the not truly needy. It turns out that the latter were the same people the Nixon administration called the working poor and saw as heroes. Reagan proceeded to reinstitute notches in various social programs such as food stamps by cutting benefits to the working poor while maintaining benefits to the truly needy who turned out primarily to be persons on welfare. In the final analysis, these changes were justified not in moral terms but rather as ways of cutting the budget that would produce the least political reaction.[17]

The final chapter in this story is a piece of legislation passed in 1988 under the leadership of Senator Daniel Patrick Moynihan. It was a mix of proposals, some considered conservative and some considered liberal but all aimed at encouraging family and work. In relation to families, one provision was designed to toughen support laws to require absent parents (mostly men) to support their children. At the same time, states were required to have AFDC-UP (Unemployed Parent), a program that allows a second parent to stay in the home rather than to leave so the family can get benefits. In relation to work, the legislation required those caring for children (usually mothers) to accept jobs or training even when the children are as young as one year old. At the same time, it encouraged states to allow welfare recipients to continue to receive some benefits and health insurance even after they get job training or employment. Again, moral principles lie at the center of this legislation, that two-parent families (or at least parental support) and work (even by single parents of young children) are good.

PRESENT STATUS

This is the story of how we came to have this complicated welfare system that no one likes. The social insurance programs—primarily Social Security and Medicare—serve a population generally considered deserving of support, mainly the elderly who worked in jobs where they paid the social security tax. These benefits are paid to recipients whether they need them or not. The programs are widely popular. A second group of programs—Food Stamps, Supplemental Security Income (SSI), and Unemployment Insurance—are a little more suspect morally but serve populations or needs widely considered legitimate. As a result, they are fully funded by the federal government, usually at more generous and secure levels. Third, there are the programs that are morally suspect—AFDC and Medicaid— which are only partially funded at the federal level. Finally, there is

General Assistance which serves the most morally suspect group and receives no federal support.

The amount of money spent on these programs by the federal government is consistent with these moral valuations. Actual outlays for each program in fiscal year 1991 were:

Social Security	$241.2 billion
Medicare	$69.6 billion
Medicaid	$52.5 billion
Unemployment Insurance	$27.1 billion
Food Stamps	$18.7 billion
SSI	$15.9 billion
AFDC	$13.5 billion[18]

Medicaid serves the recipients of both SSI and AFDC. Even recognizing that the AFDC amount is matched roughly dollar for dollar by state and local governments, it is interesting that the program that is so unpopular (AFDC) actually receives the least amount of federal money. What this may suggest is that AFDC is so controversial, not because it is expensive, but because it raises such fundamental moral issues about American society.

In each case where I have referred to the moral status of programs in the preceding review of the American welfare system, I have intended to make a factual not value statement. In other words, I was attempting to state what I think most Americans believe, not what they should believe. By the end of this book I intend to make clear just what my moral views regarding work and welfare are. These moral views will be rooted in my theology of the human condition. At this point, I hope only to have made the point clear that welfare laws are grounded in moral evaluations. If true, this means that the welfare system is a mess in part because we are so confused about the moral issues raised by poverty, work, and welfare in our society.

THE NEGATIVE INCOME TAX—A PERENNIAL POSSIBILITY

Along the way in the previous story of the development of our welfare system an idea emerged that has influenced subsequent discussions of welfare reform so deeply that it deserves some considerable attention in its own right—the negative income tax. First described around thirty years ago by free-market conservative economist Milton Friedman, the negative income tax (NIT) is a deceptively simple proposal that lays out some very basic choices for us.[19] As Friedman describes the idea, the tax system which collects from those whose incomes fall above a certain level of exemptions and deductions would pay those whose incomes fall below that level. At first it is difficult to remember that a negative tax is a sort of a double negative; the opposite of paying taxes to the government is for the government to pay benefits to someone. Friedman proposes that this negative income tax provide a 50 percent work incentive; recipients get to keep one dollar of each two they earn. Friedman would audit this program just as taxes are and eliminate all of the other government welfare bureaucracy. Since those who go to work always end up with more income under a negative income tax, he would leave the decisions about whether and how much to work up to the voluntary choice of the recipient.

If we use Friedman's idea of integrating this program into the 1992 personal income tax system, the approximate point at which a family of four begins to pay taxes is $15,000. A chart expressing Friedman's concept would look like the following:

Family's Gross Earned Income	NIT Grant to Family	Family's Total Income
$0	$ 7,500	$ 7,500
5,000	5,000	10,000
10,000	2,500	12,500
15,000	0	15,000
16,000	-100	15,900[20]

At $15,000 the family would begin paying taxes to the government, $100 at a family income of $16,000 in this example. In this example the minimum benefit is $7,500 for a family of four, the work incentive is 50 percent, and the cutoff point (where government assistance ends) is $15,000. It is a mathematical principle that one of these three factors (minimum benefit, work incentive, and cutoff point) cannot be changed without one of the others changing too. If the minimum grant is raised, the incentive must decrease or the cutoff point must rise. There is no other choice. The same is true of any changes in either of the other two factors. This basic mathematical reality is a fundamental political problem.

According to the federal government's own statistics a family of four with an income of below approximately $14,000 is poor. How can we justify a system that provides a family which has no other income and no member who should work with less than that minimum? In Friedman's example, that family would receive only $7,500. Certainly political liberals and, I suspect, most Americans cannot justify this![21] There is, of course, a simple solution, which is to raise the minimum benefit to a higher level. If we raised it to the poverty level and left the work incentive at 50 percent the comparable chart would be:

Family's Gross Earned Income	NIT Grant to Family	Family's Total Income
$ 0	$ 14,000	$ 14,000
7,000	10,500	17,500
14,000	7,000	21,000
21,000	3,500	24,500
28,000	0	28,000
29,000	-100	28,900

When the minimum benefit is $14,000 and the work incentive is 50 percent the cutoff point *must* be $28,000. Since the official poverty level is based on an emergency food budget not adequate over the long run, some have argued for a minimum benefit of more like $25,000. If the incentive were kept at 50 percent, that would produce a cutoff point of $50,000. Do we really believe that families with incomes up to $28,000 (or $50,000 in the more radical case) should receive welfare benefits? Of course not! Once again there is a solution: we can reduce the work incentive. For instance, the National Welfare Rights Organization suggested a work incentive of one-third.[22] A poverty-level minimum benefit with a one-third incentive would produce the following chart:

Family's Gross Earned Income	NIT Grant to Family	Family's Total Income
$ 0	$ 14,000	$ 14,000
3,000	12,000	15,000
9,000	8,000	17,000
15,000	4,000	19,000
21,000	0	21,000
22,000	-100	21,900

Now the question concerns the level of the incentive. Would we who are not poor go to work or work longer hours if we only got to keep one dollar out of every three we earned? Why should we expect women with children dependent upon them and few resources to draw upon to buy the car, the clothes, the lunches, and such necessities to go to work or who lack the support necessary to assure good child care or the sharing of homemaking to do so? Realists of all political persuasions are unsure that such a small work incentive will be enough to persuade people to take a job or work longer hours.

A low minimum benefit, a high cutoff point, or a low work incentive. What a bad set of choices we have. But there is a final alternative. If we could separate the poor into two groups—those who should work and those who should not—we could be tough on those who should work and generous with those who should not. There are two serious problems with this approach. First of all, who should work, and who should decide? For instance, do we believe that the mother of a child of two years of age should work, or not? I suspect we are torn over the answer to that very basic question. We, or at least our representatives, would have to decide. Second, someone literally will have to decide in each specific case into which category this particular applicant should be placed. The person who would make that decision is a welfare bureaucrat—a welfare bureaucrat. Now, we all surely know we do not like bureaucracy and bureaucrats. However, if we are to separate the poor according to whether or not they should work, we will have to tolerate a big welfare bureaucracy to do so.

MORAL QUESTIONS

What I have tried to illustrate is that the option of a negative income tax, just like the history of the welfare system, raises moral issues just as much or more than economic and political ones. What minimum support do people deserve in America? Just how high should government support go? How much incentive does it take for people to choose to work? Do we want bureaucrats deeply involved in deciding who deserves support and who does not and, if so, by what criteria? These are the kinds of questions that we will explore in some detail in what follows.

From my reading in the area of poverty and welfare, I propose that we organize our exploration of the moral issues raised by poverty and welfare under the following five ethical questions:

1. Individuality—To what extent and how can individuals be self-determining?
2. Community—To what extent and how can communities contribute to human well-being?
3. Worth—To what extent and how are human beings worthy of respect and support by their mere existence?
4. Motivation—To what extent and how can humans act on the basis of more than short-term self-interest?
5. Hope—To what extent and how are current negative patterns of interaction and power subject to change?

We have already seen these issues raised in our description of the current status of poverty and the history of poverty and of welfare as public issues in America. We turn now to four authors with very different approaches to understanding poverty and proposing policies to deal with it: Charles Murray, Lisbeth Schorr, Lawrence Mead, and Frances Fox Piven. These four approaches have been chosen both because they are influential statements and because they represent fundamentally different views of the human condition. After reviewing the basic analysis of each of the four, we shall then ask how each addresses these five ethical issues.

CHAPTER FOUR

THE VIRTUE OF BEING
POOR BUT INDEPENDENT:
CHARLES MURRAY

Charles Murray was the analyst of social policy quoted most by the Reagan administration when they attacked the welfare system. Critics of welfare read numbers in Murray's book, *Losing Ground*,[1] that appeared to confirm their view that welfare created more problems than it solved. In Murray, Reaganites thought they had found the scholar who had proved that the social programs of the sixties were a failure. Whether his conclusions were correct or not, Murray clearly articulated a popular view of poverty and welfare and of the recent history of social policy in the United States. Thus, he became the single most influential scholar of poverty and welfare during the Reagan years. At the same time, Murray represents an abiding position in the public debate about poverty and welfare, the affirmation of independent individuals operating within a free-market economy.

In *Losing Ground,* Murray's central thesis is that somewhere between 1960 and 1970 a dramatic change in views of poverty occurred. As he tells the story, we were happily living through the fifties, enjoying the postwar economic expansion and expecting people to work and support themselves. Along came elitist social critics such as Michael Harrington with a new theory of poverty which won over social scientists and federal policy experts. Murray summarizes the change in these terms:

What emerged in the mid-1960s was an almost unbroken intellectual consensus that the individualist explanation of poverty was altogether outmoded and reactionary. Poverty was not a consequence of indolence or vice. It was not the just deserts of people who didn't try hard enough. It was produced by conditions that had nothing to do with individual virtue or effort. *Poverty was not the fault of the individual but of the system.*[2]

The rest of the book is Murray's account of how this new consensus shaped social policy and of how this new social policy led to much greater social problems.

MURRAY'S HISTORY OF POVERTY AND WELFARE

As we have already noted, our basic welfare program ADC was established by the Social Security Act of 1935. However, that did not change our fundamental view of the function of welfare. ADC was intended to provide assistance to the widows of workers not covered by Social Security, a group that was supposed to shrink over time. In any event, Murray believes that all the way through the fifties the view of poverty and welfare we inherited from the Elizabethan Poor Laws reigned. Welfare was society's attempt to care for those unable to care for themselves but always was to be limited so as not to encourage laziness and vice. By the end of the decade some felt that it was becoming more permanent and beginning to include too many people.[3]

The response of the Kennedy administration to this welfare problem was an expansion of social services and job training aimed at moving people from welfare to work. However, without knowing it, Kennedy also laid the groundwork for the grand transition to come.[4] Murray attributes this grand transition to four basic causes. First, the dramatic economic growth of the sixties led us to believe that the economic pie would continue to grow. At the same time, some poverty remained unaffected by this economic growth; this came to be called structural poverty. Third, the civil rights movement moved north, becoming more radical in its analysis, especially after the civil disorders of the sixties. Finally, it became clear that the War on Poverty's community-action and job-training programs had not ended poverty. The dream that people could be moved off welfare had died.

According to Murray, an intellectual coup by a small elite happened sometime between 1964 and 1967. This small elite captured the social policy mind of the nation. He claims that thinking among the experts changed "from a view of the American system as benign and self-correcting to the pervasive assumption that if something was wrong, the system was to blame."[5] Poverty was no longer the failure of individuals within a basically healthy social and economic system. Now, poverty that persisted in spite of tremendous economic growth and the War on Poverty showed that the system itself was flawed.

One of the great ironies of Murray's account is that Richard Nixon presided over a massive expansion of welfare expenditures even though he ran against welfare and dismantled the poverty program. Many of the programs that were established under Lyndon Johnson did not really grow until Nixon was in office. Nixon's welfare reform proposal may have failed but the expansion in food stamps, health benefits, housing, work incentives, social security, and Supplemental Security Income (SSI) more than doubled the welfare budget. Parenthetically, Murray never quite fully recognizes that the Nixon administration supported most of this expansion in hopes that it would create incentives for people to move from welfare to work by providing benefits to the working poor. Later, when Reagan cut welfare it was the working poor who suffered most.

As Murray describes the period of 1950–80, when federal spending and regulation increased in the areas of poverty, employment, wages and occupations, education, crime, and the family, conditions worsened.[6] More specifically, problems in these areas increased dramatically in the seventies after the great transition in thinking he described and the resulting increases in welfare expenditures. In spite of more assistance for the poor, poverty increased through the seventies, especially if figured on the basis of income before government help. In spite of more money for job training, not only did unemployment increase but those not even looking for work (and so not officially counted as unemployed) increased more. In spite of affirmative action, African Americans without much education fell behind and those getting jobs above their experience and ability were not promoted. In spite of federal aid to schools, students and especially African American students went to school more but learned less. In spite of federal law-enforcement grants, crime rates exploded. In spite of all sorts of new government assistance to families, illegitimate births went up dramatically. All in all, someone who predicted in 1966 what the trends in these areas would be, based upon past experience, would have underestimated the problems in each case, even though billions of dollars were spent.

It is important to Murray's tale of the history of social policy that the emergence of a consensus among experts that poverty was a failure of the social system remained an elite view. Average Americans never agreed and increasingly regarded the sixties as the time when their society started falling apart. Whether they blamed welfare, permissive judges, affirmative action, busing, or rock music, Murray believes most Americans retained a common-sense commitment to individual responsibility. He summarizes this popular wisdom in three core premises:

Premise #1: People respond to incentives and disincentives. Sticks and carrots work.

Premise #2: People are not inherently hard working or moral. In the absence of countervailing influences, people will avoid work and be amoral.

Premise #3: People must be held responsible for their actions. Whether they *are* responsible in some ultimate philosophical or biochemical sense cannot be the issue if society is to function.[7]

Murray's thesis is that social policy went astray in the sixties by following the elite consensus rather than this popular wisdom, with disastrous results.

HAROLD AND PHYLLIS

How exactly did this work out in practice? Enter Harold and Phyllis.[8] Murray uses this fictitious couple to represent the typical young poor couple who are born of poor parents, who have just graduated from high school with no motivation to go to college, who are no more lazy than others, and who soon will become parents. Murray places them in Pennsylvania in 1960 and again in 1970 and asks in each case what it makes sense for them to do, given the system they encounter. Harold and Phyllis can marry or not, and Harold can get a job running a press in the dry cleaners, which is hard work at pretty low pay. What should they do?

Under the welfare rules in 1960, Harold and Phyllis could not live together, Phyllis could collect only $24 a week on AFDC (not enough to support the family of three), and if she went to work she would lose a dollar from the welfare grant for every dollar she earned. Assuming they wanted to be married, it made the most economic sense to do so and live on Harold's pay ($40 a week), and in time Phyllis might even add to the family income by taking a part-time job herself.

By 1970, the welfare regulations had changed. The Supreme Court had ruled that the welfare administration could not punish a recipient for having a man living with her. By then many states, including Pennsylvania, provided benefits to married couples if both were unemployed. A work incentive program for recipients allowed them to keep the first $30 and then one-third of the rest of their earnings if they went to work. Now Harold and Phyllis could marry and collect welfare as unemployed parents ($136 per week). Even better economically, they could remain unmarried and live together without the welfare department bothering them. If Harold also worked they could add his pay to her welfare grant. Phyllis could even get a job too and keep $30 and one-third of what she made. If Harold got tired of his hot pressing job at a local cleaners, he could quit and collect unemployment compensation and still count on Phyllis getting her welfare check. Clearly the smartest thing to do economically was not to marry, to live together, and to pool their incomes.

Murray summarizes the changes that occurred between 1960 and 1970 with the following charts, in which all of the amounts are adjusted to 1980 dollars to correct for inflation:

| | 1960 Options: Living Together | | 1970 Options: Living Together | |
	Unmarried	Married	Unmarried	Married
Harold Works	$111	$111	$270	$136
Harold Does Not Work	$0	$0	$134	$134[9]

While it was intended as a simple way to identify families where no adult could work, the exclusion of two-parent families has been criticized from all sides and recent changes have pretty well eliminated such exclusion. Similarly, midnight raids, even on poor people, to determine whether a woman is sleeping alone are hard to justify in a free society. Thus, Murray settles upon the $30-and-a-third rule as his primary target for criticism.[10]

THIRTY-AND-A-THIRD

The issue involved here is big enough to deserve more attention. Thirty-and-a-third is a good example of a policy aimed at one problem that creates another inequity. The goal was to provide a simple, noncoercive economic incentive to encourage those on welfare to take jobs and work themselves off welfare—a very widely shared goal. However, in order to save money, the only people allowed to qualify for the work incentive were those already on welfare. This made it possible for two people to be working side by side at a poverty wage but for the one of them who had previously been a full-time welfare recipient to continue to receive assistance under thirty-and-a-third while the other did not because she had never been a welfare recipient. There are two solutions to this new inequity created by thirty-and-a-third. Eliminate thirty-and-a-third as Murray advocates or adopt some version of a negative income tax system that applies to all of the poor whether or not they have ever been on welfare. The latter has been advocated by people, such as Milton Friedman, who otherwise agree more or less fully with Murray's basic view of the world. Murray suggests that the only solution to the problems with thirty-and-a-third is to eliminate it. In fact, the Earned Income Tax Credit that was enacted when thirty-and-a-third was eliminated was a small version of a negative income tax. More about the Earned Income Tax Credit will follow when we examine current policy options.

Murray argues that similar incentives developed during the same period of time, 1960–70, in the areas of crime and education.[11] The odds of getting caught and of being punished for a crime lessened, creating greater incentives to commit crimes. Deterioration in public education led to better grades for less work and fewer punishments for disrupting education, resulting in less incentive for actual learning. All of these changes in incentives reinforced one another, leading to more welfare, more single-parent families, more unemployment, more crime, and less education.

According to Murray, the final factor helping to explain the negative trends since 1960 is status.[12] Under the old understanding of poverty as a matter of personal responsibility, those poor who worked hard had status compared to those who did not. Once the cause of poverty was attributed to society rather than the individual, all of the poor had the same status; they were all victims. This homogenization of the poor reinforced by financial rewards to those not working and not marrying removed the stigma of receiving welfare, a stated goal of groups like the National Welfare Rights Organization. It became socially acceptable, and even financially rewarding, not to work. In this situation, "The man who keeps working is, in fact, a chump."[13] Without rewards of either money or status many simply quit trying to escape from poverty.

MURRAY'S GENERAL PROGRAM

What then does Murray propose we do? He believes that the first step is to determine what we are trying to accomplish. From his point of view some people deserve our support—the fifty-year-old person who has worked his or her entire life and is suddenly out of work because his or her factory closes. Others do not deserve our help—a healthy man who refuses to work. Good policy would not lump the two together; it would discriminate in favor of the person who deserves help.[14] To treat all of the poor in the same manner actually punishes the deserving in relation to the lazy. Similarly the hard-working student suffers at the hands of the troublemakers in permissive schools and the safety of the law-abiding neighbor is threatened by criminals released by soft judges. The great danger Murray sees in government transfer programs is that in an effort to provide immediate help to people in need they may create less long-term happiness. He believes there are some difficult moral choices involved that are not simply a matter of generosity versus cost cutting, but rather what is in the long-term best interest for everyone involved. He concludes that any transfer program is "inherently treacherous" and that transfers from one poor person to another poor person "are uncomfortably like robbery."[15]

On the basis of all of these considerations, Murray proposes three laws of social programs:

#1. *The Law of Imperfect Selection.* Any objective rule that defines eligibility for a social transfer program will irrationally exclude some persons.[16]

#2 *The Law of Unintended Rewards.* Any social transfer increases the net value of being in the condition that prompted the transfer.[17]

#3 *The Law of Net Harm.* The less likely it is that the unwanted behavior will change voluntarily, the more likely it is that a program to induce change will cause net harm.[18]

The first law means that programs either punish those irrationally excluded or must expand in size to try to include all those who deserve support. Thirty-and-a-third is a good example of the second law. If I must be on welfare to qualify for the work incentive, there is an incentive for me to quit my job, go on welfare, and then get a job in which I will then qualify for the thirty-and-a-third.

Murray thinks the third law is decisive. Let us assume that it is hard to get a person who has been unemployed for a long time to work beside Harold in that hot pressing job. If we create government-financed incentives significant enough to get that person to work, these incentives are likely to attract people to the government program who would otherwise work without government incentives and will lead to new inequities between recipients and other poor people who do not qualify. Thus, Murray believes, "at this point, it appears that any program that would succeed in helping large numbers of the hardcore unemployed will make hardcore unemployment a highly desirable state to be in."[19] He thinks that so far we have created the worse of both worlds. The incentives are not enough to get the hard-core unemployed to work but are enough to attract a number of people to depend on the government programs. Indeed, he states, "My conclusion is that social programs in a democratic society tend to produce net harm in dealing with the most difficult problems."[20]

On this basis Murray finally tells us what he proposes for social policy. In the area of race, Murray contends that the racial prejudice that existed before 1965 was replaced by racial condescension after then. Fueled by the elite consensus that African Americans were owed a debt for the system's failure, the intelligentsia and policy makers began "to tolerate and make excuses for behavior among blacks that whites would disdain in themselves or their children."[21] Instead, he proposes to get rid of all legislation or court decisions that allow any distinctions based on race—the end of affirmative action. For education, Murray proposes a voucher system and schools that have strong standards but allow students to repeat courses as often as they need to do to succeed.[22]

MURRAY'S WELFARE PROGRAM

Welfare is the area in which he calls for the most detailed changes.[23] He proposes the elimination of all federal programs "for working-aged persons, including AFDC, Medicaid, Food Stamps, Unemployment Insurance, Worker's Compensation, subsidized housing, disability insurance, and the rest."[24] The only federal program he would reinstate is unemployment compensation for limited periods of time to help those who have worked to make the transition to a new job. These changes will have little effect on most Americans and will reward the hard-working poor who have not turned to the government for help. It will require the dependent poor to change their behavior to fit the new reward system. Those still in need will have to turn to local voluntary charity or local government assistance, both of which Murray believes will be more subject to the specific realities of need and to the popular wisdom's commitment to self-support. In response to those who would accuse him of starving children he responds: "Hungry children should be fed; there is no argument about that. It is no less urgent that children be allowed to grow up in a system free of the forces that encourage them to remain poor and dependent."[25]

MURRAY'S CONCLUSIONS

Murray summarizes his whole approach by contending that we must return to equality of opportunity and quit trying to engineer equal outcomes. He believes that the United States does a pretty good job of rewarding effort for most of its citizens. In the case of the poor, however, government gets in the way of the reward system with disastrous results. The solution is for the government to withdraw. While this may seem mean-spirited, it is better in the long run to allow poor people to take responsibility for themselves. Well-meaning liberals who do not face this reality do more harm than good. He concludes: "When reforms finally do occur, they will happen not because stingy people have won, but because generous people have stopped kidding themselves."[26]

What we have in Charles Murray is the most recent incarnation of the free-market approach to welfare. Milton Friedman, whom we discussed in regard to earlier welfare reform, was the best-known advocate of this approach in the past.[27] They share the same basic assumption, that independent individuals are the fundamental human reality. These independent individuals seek their own interests, good or bad. They best relate to one another by trading in a free market that rewards those who produce what others want. Through competition these individuals are forced to find efficient ways to produce, leading to improvements in the standard of living of everyone. Since each individual is independent, no standards of good or bad behavior are possible except that individuals should be free to decide for themselves. When Friedman proposed a negative income tax, his primary concern was that whatever mechanism was used should help poor people preserve as much independence as possible. Murray argues that any help creates too much dependence. Both finally fall back on the competitive market as the best guarantee of self-sufficiency.

In describing Murray's position, I have suggested some moral implications of his perspective. Now, it is time to get much more serious and organized about the moral dimension of his work. As I have already suggested, poverty and welfare policy raise five fundamental ethical issues.

INDIVIDUALITY

The self-determining individual is the bottom line of Murray's analysis. He believes that our market economy and free society work pretty well to provide opportunity for individuals who want to get ahead. He concludes:

> In short, American society is very good at reinforcing the investment of an individual in himself. For the affluent and for the middle-class, these mechanisms continue to work about as well as they ever have, and we enjoy their benefits.[28]

This is as it should be. The goal of policy should be to allow individuals to decide their own destiny. The independent, choosing agent is the final reality. Other than supporting themselves and making their own choices, Murray prefers to make no qualitative judgments about what individuals do. Any attempt to evaluate the choices people make is likely to deteriorate into paternalism, which improperly assumes that I know better than you what you should do and undermines your capacity to decide for yourself.

COMMUNITY

This assumption that the fundamental reality is the independent individual has implications for Murray's view of community. At its best the community is for him just a collection of self-determining individuals.

Individuals decide what to make of their social environment. Indeed our social policies went wrong precisely at the point where the elite decided that the community determined the individual's fate. When the government got involved in trying to change the social factors, it merely undermined the self-determination of the poor:

> American government, in its recent social policy, has been ineffectual in trying to stage-manage their decision to invest [in themselves], and it has been unintentionally punitive toward those who would make the decision on their own. It is time to get out of their way.[29]

Obviously, he thinks the poor essentially can solve their own problems in spite of the social context.

WORTH

"Some people are better than others. They deserve more of society's rewards, of which money is only one small part."[30] Thus does Murray state clearly his view that people must earn the right to be respected. How he thinks this happens is not clear, but he is convinced that some people of all income levels have the initiative to get ahead. The excuse that some people have been born into a social situation that handicaps the development of such initiative is but the failed elite view of the sixties. Rather, he believes the government should simply get out of the way so that the market system can provide its reward to the motivated. He concludes: "Government cannot identify the worthy, but it can protect a society in which the worthy can identify themselves."[31] What of the unworthy? They will have to learn to be motivated the hard way or depend upon the minimal assistance available from private charity and local government. As he stated in his third premise of the popular wisdom: "Whether they *are* responsible in some ultimate philosophical or biochemical sense cannot be the issue if society is to function."[32] Clearly, Murray believes that people must earn their place in the world and that any attempt to help them make it merely creates more problems in the long run.

MOTIVATION

The first two premises of the popular wisdom Murray contrasts to the elite theory both speak to human motivation. The first says that people respond to incentives, and the second states that people tend to be lazy and immoral. For Murray, the only real corrective to these human tendencies is the harsh reality of the marketplace. There we learn that we had better work and rein in our immorality or we shall fail. This has worked well for most Americans and even for poor Americans until the sixties. Then, all of a sudden, "it became socially acceptable within poor communities to be unemployed, because working families too were receiving welfare."[33] The distinctions between good, working people and bad, unemployed have been broken down, and money being available to support those who did not work meant people no longer had to work either for income or for status. The intrinsic good of work is a distant philosophic concept. "The man who keeps working is, in fact, a chump."[34]

HOPE

Finally, there is the question of hope. Here Murray is honest and direct:

> The tangible incentives that any society can realistically hold out to the poor
> youth . . . are mostly penalties, mostly disincentives. "Do not study, and we will
> throw you out; commit crimes and we will put you in jail; do not work, and we

will make sure that your existence is so uncomfortable that any job will be preferable to it." To promise much more is a fraud.[35]

Murray does not overpromise. He assumes Harold can expect little more than that hot job as a presser in the cleaners for the rest of his life. Yet, Murray asks whether readers would not prefer their children to be raised in Harold's family with him working at that job rather than by a family on welfare. To Murray, the choice is clear, but it probably says even more about him that this is the only choice he can imagine for young people like Harold and Phyllis. For Murray, to lead them to hope for more would be dishonest.

It is this basic reality—that life is not fair and is not easy, especially if you are born poor—that the elite concept tried to deny. Popular wisdom recognizes that individuals are responsible for making their way in this world. Any attempt by society to take some responsibility for the destiny of the poor merely encourages them to withdraw from the harsh real world and punishes those trying to do their best in that tough real world. Government needs to get out of the way and let motivated people make the best of what they have.

CONCLUSION

Charles Murray is the voice of the conservative individualistic analysis of poverty and welfare policy. His central principle is individual freedom unfettered by government intervention. For him, community is but a collection of individuals, people must earn their own way in life, self-interest is the only dependable motivation, and there is little reason to believe that poverty will end any time soon. Consistent with these principles, Murray sees poverty as personal failure reinforced all too often by bad incentives provided by government programs. The only welfare program that would fit with these ethical commitments is no welfare. Individuals should be left to their own devices or the charity of their family and neighbors.

CHAPTER FIVE

DEVELOPING COMPETENT PEOPLE: LISBETH SCHORR

Lisbeth Schorr represents the typical American impulse when faced with a social issue—to get involved directly in helping the individuals affected. She shares Murray's emphasis on the individual but has a very different view of how individuals become independent. Murray believes motivated individuals must struggle in the competitive market to control their destiny. Success or failure depends primarily on how much effort each of us is willing to give. Lisbeth Schorr believes that individuals are shaped decisively by their place in the society. Success or failure depends significantly on the accident of birth, not just the willpower of the person. Whereas Murray wants government to stay out of the way, Schorr believes the government must provide supportive services to help those who were born into poverty to develop into motivated, competent human beings. Murray accepts individuals as they are and leaves them on their own; Schorr seeks to help individuals develop into the people they can be.

Perhaps Schorr best expresses this difference between herself and those like Murray in discussing the purpose of her book, *Within Our Reach*:

> The drama of success chronicled in this book is not the drama of *beating* the odds, but the drama of *changing* the odds. While there are heroes and heroines whose life stories stir us because, as a result of extraordinary individual endowment, they have been able to triumph over adversity that would cripple more ordinary youngsters, this book is not their story. Rather, it is the story of how our society can raise the chances that millions of ordinary children, growing up

75

in circumstances that make them vulnerable, will develop into healthy and productive adults.[1]

Murray wants to make sure we reward those who beat the odds rather than punish them as he believes current welfare policy does. Schorr wants to provide the assistance necessary to help most poor people make it.

SCHORR'S ANALYSIS

Schorr's book, *Within Our Reach*, is based on two overarching theses. The first is that we know how to change the odds of success for children at risk. She contends that there are successful programs of social services that address the various threats to vulnerable children. Contrary to those who argue that the underclass is beyond help, she says the evidence is clear that poor families and children can be helped from the outside. Much of her book is a set of case studies of specific examples of such successful social services.[2] Second, she is convinced that all Americans have a stake in what happens to poor children. She argues:

> We all pay to support the unproductive and incarcerate the violent. We are all economically weakened by lost productivity. We all live with fear of crime in our homes and on the streets. We are all diminished when large numbers of parents are incapable of nurturing their dependent young, and when pervasive alienation erodes the national sense of community.[3]

In part, she is contending that the cost of supportive social services is less than the cost of failure—a simple monetary cost-benefit analysis. But in part she is also arguing that we should factor in nonmonetary values.

Schorr does recognize the role of economic policy. Economic growth, jobs, and job training that makes possible work which pays enough to support a family are essential to dealing with poverty. However, these will never be enough without adequate social services to help high-risk children and families benefit from that work.[4] So Schorr recognizes that both are needed. However, she then writes a book entirely about the social service programs, not about basic economic opportunity. At the end of the book she concludes: "In the next decade's efforts to break the cycle of disadvantage and dependence, first priority must go to making intensive, high quality services available early in the life cycle to the populations at highest risk."[5] It is clear, then, that while Schorr recognizes the importance of broader economic opportunity, her personal stress is on social services to help individuals and families succeed. This separates her from those who believe that society must be changed fundamentally before poverty will ever end.

It is fair to say that Schorr holds to the view that Murray attributes to the elite of the sixties: society, not the individual, is primarily responsible for poverty. Schorr responds directly to Murray.[6] He is, by her account, simply wrong in believing that welfare causes social problems. The real cause of the growth in poverty is the lack of economic growth in the seventies, which would have made matters even worse without the success of the antipoverty programs of the sixties which Murray criticizes. In her view, the government has done too little, not too much.

Assistance for the elderly has expanded dramatically without the same sort of political criticism as that for young families. The reason she gives for this difference in acceptance is key:

> It is almost impossible to help poor children without helping their families, and we worry that support to young families—especially with financial assistance—will rob them of their incentive to work, sap their motivation to be responsible parents, and encourage casual sex, early and multiple childbearing, and endless cycles of dependency.[7]

Contrary to Murray, Schorr thinks careful research shows that public assistance has not made things worse and that other programs, the social services she advocates, have made things better. It is those better programs that we must expand. She seems a little unclear about the value dimension of this debate, which we discovered when we examined the history of our welfare system. We support assistance for older Americans and for children because most Americans do not blame them for their poverty. Yet, these poor children usually live with poor adults whom most Americans do blame for their poverty. Moral judgment drives political choices to the detriment of the children. Schorr ignores this reality.

Schorr does address another values debate directly. Many believe that poverty results from failures of character and family values that cannot be influenced by government policy. However, she believes "social policy can significantly strengthen or weaken a family's ability to instill virtue in its children."[8] All families get help from health services, schools, churches, and neighbors; but families with children at risk for failure need particular help to be the parents their children need. Schorr believes persons of a wide range of political persuasions can unify around this goal of helping today's vulnerable children become competent adults. She believes that the successful programs she has studied provide the ideas necessary to reach this goal.

WHAT IS AT STAKE?

Before turning to those specific programs, Schorr tries to detail the costs of failure and key risk factors. Important costs she identifies are youth crime, school dropout, and young childbearing. In each area she reviews all of the data on the price to both the people involved and to society for these problems, all of which correlate highly with being born and raised in poverty. Interestingly Murray and Schorr agree on what the problems are and that they are getting worse. Drugs, declining wages, and deteriorating neighborhoods make these problems more intense and more difficult for individuals to solve.

While each of these problems can be described separately, they overlap and reinforce one another in everyday life and are concentrated in specific geographic areas. As serious as this reality is, only about 1 percent of the U.S. population lives in census tracts with particularly high levels of all of these problems. Thus, the number of children growing up in such neighborhoods is "small enough that intensive efforts to serve these children and their families would be manageable—and high enough that inaction is intolerable."[9]

High-risk is a term professionals use to describe kids who have the odds stacked against them. Various factors can be listed as risks. Schorr identifies five areas of risk: unwanted births, babies born with health problems, children in poor health, children neglected or abused, and educational failure. On the basis of her research Schorr concludes:

> Three clear themes emerge: First, *risk factors leading to later damage occur more frequently among children in families that are poor* and still more frequently among

families that are persistently poor and live in areas of concentrated poverty. Second, *the plight of the children bearing these risks is not just individual and personal;* it requires a societal response. Third, *the knowledge to help is available;* there is a reasonably good match between known risk factors and the interventions to reduce them.[10]

Success in reducing any of the risk factors increases the odds that high-risk kids will succeed. Coordinated efforts in each area will have much greater impact. Schorr then proceeds to describe in much more interesting detail than this summary allows successful programs addressing each of the five areas of risk.

PROGRAMS THAT WORK

In the case of teenage pregnancy, Schorr is a strong advocate of widely available, government-supported birth control.[11] She argues that subsidized family planning played a major role in reducing unwanted births and infant mortality. The Reagan administration attacked family planning in part out of their opposition to abortion and in part from capitulation to right-wing sexual moralism. Precisely because the growing problem of unmarried teenage pregnancy comes from a mix of lack of information and the confused motivation of young women looking for the love missing in their lives, Schorr's basic solution is school-based birth-control clinics that are uniquely placed both to provide the technology and to help young people struggle with their needs and motivations. Such clinics are quite controversial in large part because the need for them is an admission that times have changed. Media advocacy of sex has overpowered families and churches; especially in poor neighborhoods, "marriageable" men are hard to find; failure in school increasingly predicts failure in later life. In the long run, young people must see hope in their lives and see the connection between preventing an unwanted pregnancy and that hope. Schorr is convinced that school-based clinics can bring the practical technology together with these educational and personal needs.

Babies born prematurely, of low birth-weight, or of addicted mothers, start out behind and many never catch up.[12] Not only is this a human tragedy, but it is also extremely expensive for all of us.

Preventive prenatal care promises to reduce both the human and financial costs before children are born. Usually the mothers involved are very young and inexperienced; frequently they do not want to admit they are pregnant; all too often they are pregnant from sexual abuse or incest. For all of these reasons, many young women do not seek the medical care they need during their pregnancies. Schorr describes in detail programs in California, Baltimore, and South Carolina that try to take the prenatal care to the women who need it.

The health needs of poor children certainly do not end at birth.[13] Such children grow up in neighborhoods with particular hazards from both disease and the environment, for example ear infections and peeling lead paint. Again the costs are both human and monetary. For instance, a high percentage of both school dropouts and young people convicted of crime had significant health problems as young children. Again, those in the most need are the least likely to get help. Parents may have personal problems of their own or may not qualify for Medicaid. Lack of transportation or lack of money for prescriptions may keep even motivated parents from getting help for their kids. Often solutions to the health problems require social or environmental change—for example, clean water—more than traditional health care. Schorr describes specific programs in Mississippi, Baltimore, and the Watts area of Los Angeles, which take medical care to the children in the neighborhoods, with dramatic positive results.

The problems of prenatal and child health care raise the more general problem of gaps in our national health care system.[14] At present a wide range of special programs seek to fill those gaps—Medicaid; Early and Periodic Screening, Diagnosis, and Treatment (ESDT); Supplemental Food for Women, Infants, and Children (WIC); and federal support for neighborhood clinics. Studies have shown the preventive value of these programs, and Schorr at least advocates the expansion of them. However, holes remain and with health costs going up so quickly all health programs are stressing cost containment. The result is irrational regulations in both private and public health insurance such as Medicaid paying only for the most expensive mental health care for children—psychiatric care. Schorr advocates a national health insurance program that includes at least the following three elements:

• Universal access to the health care system.

- Ways of paying for services that would make possible some rational alloca-
tion of health resources.
- Systematic attention to the content of services and the circumstances in
which they are provided, taking into full account the special needs of
disadvantaged families.[15]

She believes these criteria can be met without forcing a uniformity
upon disparate health needs.

While some of her policy proposals in these health areas may be
controversial, Americans generally agree about preventing unwanted
pregnancies and about providing health care to pregnant women and
to children. Americans are much less sure about what they think
about families.[16] Some of us urge public agencies to get tougher in
enforcing laws against child abuse and neglect while others blame
youth crime on laws against child abuse, which they believe meddle
in the parents' right to discipline their children. Often the same
people hold both views. Should government get involved in families
that are not raising children well, and will government help if it does?
Schorr clearly thinks government can and must intervene for the sake
of the children. Lack of money, lack of family and neighborhood
support, youth and inexperience, and personal problems of their own
can lead parents to be unable to help their child develop normally or
to actual abuse or neglect. The increase in poverty, young mothers,
single-parent families, and drug abuse compounds these problems.
According to Schorr, too many families in trouble simply do not
provide the love children need, with disastrous long-term results.

Like the problem of families, programs to provide support for
them are quite different and complicated. One program in Tacoma,
Washington, which Schorr describes, involves intensive therapy over
an extended period of time in the homes of parents about to lose their
children because of abuse or neglect. She concludes that the program
has succeeded in helping parents become self-sufficient, capable
parents at a cost far below foster care and psychiatric care. A program
in New Haven using pediatricians and social workers provides many
similar services for mothers while featuring child care for the children. A visiting nurses program in Elmira, New York, represents yet
another approach to intensive long-term support for parents. All have
in common high-intensity services dealing with the full range of family
needs, which are taken to the homes of the families. They look

expensive until compared to the alternatives. The real question, according to Schorr, is whether we are willing to support families whose lives are at risk as much as babies or old people for whom we provide very expensive intensive health care. Thus far we have not been.

Finally, Schorr turns to the education of children. The need for early childhood education has increased dramatically with most women now in the workforce, many young mothers who should be in school themselves, and the growing consensus that welfare recipients should work.[17] The great danger is that in the rush to provide child care we will forget that education during the first five years of life is critical to success later in life. The positive side of this danger is that evidence is clear that early childhood education can make such a positive difference that investments in it pay off. This is the basic justification for Head Start, the federal program that provides comprehensive early childhood education including health and nutrition and social services, primarily for low-income children. Head Start's central goal is to help those children catch up to the educational advantages of the more affluent. Schorr concludes that research by a number of different groups has documented the value of Head Start better than any other program she discusses. Thus, fully funding Head Start so it can reach all eligible children is one step she supports strongly.[18]

Fully funding Head Start still leaves many children, especially those under four, in need of child care of the same educational quality. Stress must be placed on the needs of the children at least as much as those of the parents. While Schorr believes a variety of mechanics can be used to accomplish this, she proposes six guiding principles for child care: it must be targeted on the poorest children, Head Start and similar programs must be expanded, funding adequate to provide quality care is essential, parents must be partners, schools must become a major source of preschool education, and a broad range of support for these services is essential.

Last of all, Schorr takes on elementary schools, which she calls the "balance wheel of the social machinery."[19] We have believed that universal public education would provide the equality of opportunity upon which America prides itself. It is increasingly clear that the opposite is the case, that the problems of the schools many poor children attend make it very difficult for them to succeed in the adult world. Compensatory education has proved that it can help turn around school performance, although it has less effect after third grade. Once children come to see themselves as failures, it is harder and harder to reach them. Schorr describes the schools in New Haven with which James Comer has worked, schools in Prince Georges County, Maryland, patterned after the New Haven experience, and a school in East Harlem as successful examples of schools that reach low-income kids. All stress cooperation among parents, teachers, and staff; warmth and love in the classrooms; and attention to the specific needs of individual children. Comer adds to this a lot of special services from social workers to psychologists to health care. In every case student performance has shown significant improvement.

BUILDING ON SUCCESSFUL PROGRAMS

What are the marks of all these programs Schorr has described as successfully addressing the key risks faced by poor children? They typically offer a broad spectrum of services that cross traditional professional and bureaucratic lives. They view the child "in the context of the family and the family in the context of its surroundings."[20] They care about those they serve and reach out to them to make the services easy to use. She summarizes these traits in the following terms:

> In short, the programs that succeed in helping the children and families in the shadows are intensive, comprehensive, and flexible. They also share an extra dimension, more difficult to capture: Their climate is created by skilled, committed professionals who establish respectful and trusting relationships and respond to the individual needs of those they serve. The nature of their services, the terms on which they are offered, the relationships with families, the essence of the programs themselves—all take their shape from the needs of those they serve rather than from the precepts, demands, and boundaries set by professionalism and bureaucracies.[21]

In sum, successful programs place the persons being served at the center of their attention and do not let anything get in the way of delivering that service.

On the other hand programs that fail to help poor children, which are more common than those that succeed, simply do not approach their job in the same way. Sadly, when they fail we blame that failure on the poor children and conclude that they are beyond help. Schorr counters this pessimistic view:

> Many interventions have turned out to be ineffective . . . because we have tried to attack complex, deeply rooted tangles of troubles with isolated fragments of help, with help rendered grudgingly in one-shot forays, with help designed less to meet the needs of beneficiaries than to conform to professional or bureaucratic convenience.[22]

There is no reason to believe that these complex problems can be solved by simple, middle-class, or cheap solutions. Yet, we keep trying such solutions and investing a lot of money in them.

How, then, do we generalize upon these successful programs? To do so, we must know what works, prove we can afford it, attract good personnel, resist diluting the programs, cut down on bureaucracy, and use different strategies for replication.[23] Schorr responds to each of these six challenges by citing statistics that show results from the programs. She argues that these preventive programs will save money in the long run both in each particular problem area and in other areas too. For example, healthy kids have fewer health problems later and do better in school. She believes idealistic professionals will be drawn to programs successfully addressing significant human needs. She thinks it is clear that diluted programs will fail and that people can be brought to understand that. Similarly, she assumes legislators and administrators will come to see that bureaucracies must get out of the way. Finally, the structure is already established for replicating some programs such as Head Start on a national scale. In other cases, state and local organizations need to study various successful programs and then figure out the best specific program for their area.

Schorr pulls together all of her analysis into one final appeal. Now that we have successful programs which are addressing all of the risk areas she identified, we no longer can claim that there is nothing we can do about the fate of poor children. The costs of not doing something to improve the odds of success for these children is increasingly obvious, all of which leads Schorr to conclude, "In the next decade's efforts to break the cycle of disadvantage and dependence, first priority must go to making intensive, high quality services available early in the life cycle to the populations at highest risk."[24] We will all pay a high price for failure to do so. Now, we are in a much better position to see much more specifically how Schorr would respond to the five ethical questions that arose as we analyzed Murray.

INDIVIDUALITY

Like Murray, Schorr focuses upon the individual poor person, specifically the poor child. The fundamental difference is that she does not believe people can be self-determining as easily as Murray seems to think. Rather, they are shaped by their experiences in decisive ways and poor children face particular obstacles to growing into self-determining adults. The social services she proposes are designed to bring new influences into the lives of poor children, making it more possible for them to *develop into* the self-determining adults Murray prizes. Murray basically says that poor people should be left alone to make their own way in the market, whereas Schorr argues that poor people at least need help if they are to be able to succeed in that market.

Murray and groups composed of poor people would both challenge Schorr about channeling large amounts of money to relatively well-off professionals (doctors, teachers, social workers, etc.) instead of to the poor people themselves. These professionals are then basically going to be telling the poor people how to live their lives. Murray would argue that this will lead to poor people being dependent upon these professionals rather than determining their own lives. Poor people's advocates would argue that the money should go straight to the poor people who need it, not to middle-class professionals. Schorr would respond that poor people, and especially poor children, need good professional help in order to become self-determining.

COMMUNITY

As I suggested at the beginning of this analysis of Schorr, she notes the need for fundamental social change. Practically, this comes down to the importance of jobs and income for all. Yet, throughout the discussion of specifics she ignores any reference to economic policy, job training, or other employment strategies. She also ignores the growing separation of Americans by race and income in where we live, which largely determines where we go to school. In stating that her social service programs have top priority in the coming decade, she puts these issues about structure of the overall society on a back burner.

The questions are obvious: Where will the children who are helped by Schorr's social service programs get jobs? and Can these programs succeed on a broad scale if poor children continue to live in one neighborhood and go to its school while well-off children live in another neighborhood and go to its school? Can we truly change the odds of success for individuals without fundamentally changing the structure of the community? While Schorr recognizes the validity of these questions in theory, in practice she largely ignores them.

WORTH

Schorr's approach to the issue of worth is popular among liberals today. She focuses on children. Who can blame children for being born poor? They have not refused to work or had children they could not support. Do they not deserve an opportunity in life just as much as those children who just happen to have been born to parents with more money? The problem, of course, is that these children almost always live with adults who behave in ways that most Americans find objectionable.

Schorr finesses these objections by constantly focusing on the children, yet her social services would often go to adults. Obviously she believes that these adults deserve support and can change their behavior if help is given; her proposals for birth control clearly illustrate this. However, her focus on the children allows her to ignore the matter that most clearly raises this ethical question of worth—work. Nevertheless, Schorr recognizes the essential worth of those who are to receive her social services and believes that such basic respect is essential to successful programs.

MOTIVATION

Psychologists distinguish between positive and negative reinforcement when they study behavior. Laboratory rats who receive consistent rewards for making the correct turn learn to run a maze; those who are punished for making the wrong turn may learn to run the maze or may give up in frustration. Murray says that we should let people pay the price of their mistakes and learn from that. It is a tough world out there in the market; the government had better not try to soften that reality, or it will create dependency. Schorr believes that given positive support poor children and their parents can develop a positive sense of self and learn to run the maze of life. This positive view of human nature particularly stresses nonmonetary rewards, like love and respect. The poor are poor not because they are greedy or bad but rather because they have not received enough love and support. Schorr's social services are designed to fill that gap.

When it comes to trying to sell her program to the nonpoor, Schorr again stresses nonmonetary factors. "To know what is worth investing in, we must include in our calculations enduring human values such as altruism, community, and justice."[25] Having said that, Schorr goes on to focus at length on the monetary benefits of her program. She makes the case that her program is a smart investment that will save money in the long run. Thus, it is in the self-interest of those who are not poor to pay taxes for prevention now rather than for welfare and prisons later. She appeals to our collective greed, contending that we can all be better off by doing good. Yet, in the final analysis she thinks the nonpoor, like the poor, will respond to positive possibilities. She concludes: "The benefits of living in a fair and just society with a shared sense of civility and community cannot be reduced to a dollar figure."[26]

HOPE

Perhaps the central message Schorr intends to send is hope. She rightly realizes that many Americans may want to do something about poverty but are not sure anything can be done. Indeed, Murray's main point seems to be that we cannot do anything positive except get out of the way. Schorr argues, quite to the contrary, that we have programs which have shown results in solving the key problems of poor children. The odds for poor children can be changed, and we know how to do it. The question is whether this message can get out to enough Americans that they will support the effort to replicate these programs throughout the country. She has confidence that if that happens, the end to poverty is in fact within our reach. As I suggested earlier she does not address along the way how our economy will create enough jobs or how our society will overcome racial, gender, and income divisions.

What we have in Lisbeth Schorr is the typical modern liberal. She stresses human development based upon positive motivation and the expectation that things can get better. All of this is facilitated by well-educated professionals using their knowledge and their accepting love to provide the supports missing in poor children's lives. Support for her program is made easier by focusing on children whose motives are more pure and who seem to have the potential for great change. In the final analysis, the object of change remains the individual who is to be helped to become an effective, functioning adult. Whether this can be done without creating dependency and without significant social change remains to be seen.

CONCLUSION

Lisbeth Schorr represents the typical approach of American liberals. She seeks to reach out and support people in trouble so that they can become capable adults. For her, community should provide this support to its members because they are of inherent worth. We should act out of both human empathy and long-term self-interest. If we do, we can end the worst aspects of poverty. Based upon these ethical convictions, Schorr views poverty primarily as the failure of society to provide the context in which people can become self-supporting. Consistent with this analysis, she advocates various direct social service programs designed to provide the support that society is failing to provide now.

CHAPTER SIX

BEHAVING LIKE A GOOD POOR CITIZEN: LAWRENCE MEAD

The Reagan conservative coalition was composed of two very different strands of thought. The libertarian strand believes that less government is better. They want to leave individuals free to make their own decisions within a free market. A second strand of conservatism, the authoritarian, does not trust individuals to make the right choice. They want government to guide or to force at least some citizens to do what is right. Even though these two strands of conservative thought are mutually exclusive in principle, most Americans who consider themselves conservative probably agree with each at different times. They may want less government when it comes to taxes, environmental regulation, and welfare, but may want more when it comes to abortion rights, school prayer, and pornography. Reagan's political genius was based in part in his ability to keep both of these two strands of conservatism in his coalition.[1] For the sake of understanding the welfare debate, we must separate them.

In the welfare policy debate, Charles Murray represents the libertarian strand of conservatism. He defends his position with appeals to less government, more market, and more individual choice. Lawrence Mead represents the authoritarian strand of conservatism. Whereas Murray would let the market discipline people, Mead believes that the government must determine what behavior is appropriate and then require citizens to behave in that way. Not only is this an abiding position in political philosophy, but it probably represents the views of most Americans about welfare policy. Indeed, in recent years some states have begun to design welfare policy based upon

Mead's analysis.[2] As a result, any attempt to understand contemporary trends in welfare policy had better come to terms with Lawrence Mead.

MEAD'S BASIC ANALYSIS

Mead worked at the Department of Health, Education, and Welfare and the Urban Institute where he observed the various work requirements included in our welfare programs. From this experience he concluded that the federal government must toughen up its work requirements. He summarizes this position in these terms:

> I think the main problem with the welfare state is its *permissiveness*, not its size. Today poverty often arises from the functioning problems of the poor themselves, especially difficulties in getting through school, working, and keeping their families together. But the social programs that support the needy rarely set standards for them. Recipients seldom have to work or otherwise function *in return* for support. If they did, the evidence suggests they would function better, bringing closer an integrated society.[3]

This view of social policy has led him to reflect more generally about human nature and the proper function of government. He goes back to Hobbes and the need for public order to begin his argument: "Civility is essential to a humane society, but it is not a natural condition, as Americans tend to assume. It is something societies must achieve, in part through public authority."[4] This civility is fundamental to the social order, which is the central value for Mead's position. He admires the more ordered society of Great Britain and worries about the possible disintegration of our own society. Social order requires citizens who function in ways consistent with the social norms of the mainstream society. Social programs are not just a means for providing assistance, they are also an opportunity to integrate recipients into mainstream social norms.

Poverty, then, is more a problem of social separation than of money. "A class of Americans, heavily poor and nonwhite, exists apart from the social mainstream."[5] This separation is what he means by a social problem, and integrating these people into the mainstream is what he looks for in solutions. The question, then, is not whether government programs provide too much assistance so much as whether they demand enough of recipients in meeting the same social norms for functioning as nonrecipients. Except in government programs, society requires certain behavior, such as work, in return for support. Government programs must do the same. If not, even those not on government assistance will begin to lose faith in the general social norms, as seems already to have begun to occur as seen in a decline in work effort by the nonpoor. In the short run this will mean a loss of freedom, but in the long run it will bring about social integration.

THE GREAT SOCIETY

Mead tells a somewhat different story of the Great Society than does Murray but reaches a very similar conclusion overall. Conservatives say the Great Society did too much for the poor; liberals say it did not do enough. According to Mead, both miss the point. The most important question is not how much assistance government gives to the poor so much as it is what government demands in return from the recipient. Like Murray, Mead blames a sociological approach for much of this failure.[6] He contends that after 1960 it became more and more difficult to identify social barriers that were keeping the poor down. Rather, it became increasingly clear that the functioning of the poor themselves was keeping them poor. The sociological approach blames social disadvantage for this failure to function, justifying even more benefits and supporting services. Obviously, Schorr's is the kind of analysis Mead has in mind in this criticism. He says this sociological approach views problems from the point of view of the poor and shifts responsibility to society, government, and the wealthy elite.

Mead largely agrees with Murray that the result of the Great Society programs was to confirm in recipients the view that they are not responsible for their own poverty. It made female-headed households economically viable and did not seriously require work in return for benefits. The resulting permissive paternalism robbed the poor of their responsibility for their own lives. "The recipients were exempted from the pressures to perform that normally emanate from schools, neighborhoods, and workplaces."[7] In a society where people must exercise such responsibility to function in the mainstream, this approach freezes the recipient in second-class citizenship just as surely,

91

if less obviously, than racial discrimination. The only solution is for government to exercise authority by requiring people to behave in the generally accepted manner. Such exercise of government authority is quite literally un-American, because we are suspicious of government telling people how to live.

WORK AND WELFARE

In many cases, government may want people to work much more than the people do themselves. This is especially true for dirty, low-paying jobs, say working in a laundry. According to Mead, many such jobs are available but people will not take them or will not keep them very long. Perhaps the poor are better off economically on assistance or working in the underground economy or both. Perhaps they are making a political statement about the unfairness of the system. Perhaps they just do not value work highly or at least highly enough to go to the trouble of getting job training, finding a job, arranging day care, and so forth necessary actually to go to work. In any event he concludes: "For recipients, work must be viewed, not as an expression of self-interest, but as an obligation owed to society."[8] Yet our American individualism leads us to want people to work out of self-interest. We want people freely to choose to work; for low-wage jobs, that is increasingly unlikely. "If society seriously wants more of the disadvantaged to work regularly, to achieve goals like integration, then it must require them to."[9]

Government has sought to find a welfare policy that creates non-coercive incentives for work. He describes what happens in the real world as a negotiation in which welfare recipients want more meaningful and well-paying jobs and society is refusing to guarantee income without an effort to work. If government learns to take society's concerns seriously, it will recognize that part of its function is "to make *obligatory* the norms that people commonly affirm but do not reliably obey."[10] This will require more government, not less. However, if government lives up to its responsibility to society, then the negotiations with recipients may well lead to requiring work while upgrading jobs. While this may involve less personal freedom in the short run, it may also lead to the capacity for independence that is essential to long-term freedom and to social order.

It is in discussing the failure to reform the welfare system that Mead introduces the position he later develops as his own, the civic conception.[11] In the congressional debates sparked by Nixon's proposals for welfare reform and later Carter's, the dominant issue that emerged was how welfare interacted with work. Liberal reformers argued for a guaranteed income high enough to sustain an adequate standard of living. They found the proposals of both Nixon and Carter inadequate primarily because the basic benefits guaranteed nationally were too low. Traditional conservatives opposed both reform proposals because they expanded government by establishing a national welfare minimum that would increase benefits significantly, especially in the Southern states. However, the decisive questions were raised by some legislators usually considered conservative like Senator Russell Long of Louisiana and many usually considered liberal like Representative Martha Griffiths of Michigan. They shared in common a simple question: why should recipients not be required to work? Griffiths particularly pointed out that with most American women working outside the home it was time to expect the same of welfare recipients. In the course of this debate and others, the Democrats became labeled as the party of permissiveness. Republicans claimed the role of authoritarians but because of their prior commitment to smaller government refused to use that authority to require the necessary changes in behavior.[12]

WORK REQUIREMENTS IN PRACTICE

Of course, welfare law did officially require recipients to work primarily through the Work Incentive (WIN) program, enacted in 1957. Mead charges, however, that welfare administrators were never willing in practice to use the power they had to enforce work. In its early years WIN emphasized job training, but in 1971 the stress was changed to immediate placement in jobs. Work requirements attached to Food Stamps, Unemployment Insurance and Disability, were always weaker than those in AFDC. Even the AFDC requirements faced difficult structural problems. The legislation was vague and top administrators never fully supported a program forced upon them by Congress. The only leverage the welfare administrators had was the benefit itself and many front-line caseworkers focused more on the needs of children and mothers than the work effort mostly of men. Finally, employers often resented the government regulations and low work effort they experienced with the program. To be effective, law and enforcement must be congruent with general public opinion; this was never true of WIN.[13]

Mead proposes a reform of the WIN program to shift it from the sociological view that recipients are disadvantaged to the civic view that they have the responsibility to their society of working. Specifically, he calls for changes in the law to define mothers as employable when their youngest child reaches three, to require them to arrange their own day care to be paid by welfare, to shorten appeals procedures, and to increase the potential sanction to the family's entire benefit, not just that of the person who refuses to work. This is to be coupled with administrative changes to require welfare agencies to double the percent of recipients in WIN, tighten up the requirement that clients cooperate, and supervise them much more closely. The real question for Mead is whether the politicians have the will to follow through on such a program.[14]

Through his own study of effective and ineffective WIN programs, Mead identified some characteristics of effective programs that sound surprisingly like Schorr's marks of effective social service programs. They were staffed by highly motivated personnel, cut through bureaucracy, were close to the neighborhoods, informal about rules and staff hierarchy, and fit programs to the people.[15] However, they were also marked by a commitment to Mead's civic approach. Personnel in those offices believed government had a right to require people to work and that it was good for the recipients in the long run. As a result, they did not accept as readily excuses about why a person could not work or a job was beneath them. Indeed, they sold the recipients on the value of work and the reasonableness of a work requirement. He concludes:

> To overcome nonwork, WIN offices must be demanding of clients. They must also be affirming. And there is no contradiction. Demands themselves are an affirmation to the clients that they actually can realize mainstream norms like work.[16]

Once again the key is government authoritatively enforcing mainstream behavior.

AMERICA'S POLITICAL PHILOSOPHY

If the civic approach is as mainstream as Mead describes, why has Washington not enacted it? First, there is the Constitution and the Supreme Court. Both are essentially liberal in Mead's sense of the term, stressing rights instead of obligations. Second, federal politicians particularly are geared up to provide benefits, not enforce demands, particularly when they move into areas of personal behavior rather than economic policy. Finally, the policy experts are dominated by economic and sociological thinking. The economists look for some economic incentive system for making low-wage work appeal to people's self-interest. The sociologists emphasize the inadequacy of government programs measured against the social disadvantages faced by poor people. These two approaches merge in proposals for some additional benefits to create incentives for work. Throughout, the emphasis of the entire system is on rights entitlements rather than obligations. According to Mead these attitudes and concepts must change if policy is to improve.

Enter the political scientist, or more correctly the political philosopher, to set things right. What we have here according to Mead the political philosopher are various versions of liberalism all failing to recognize that politics is finally about authority. Those we call conservatives oppose all authority especially that of the government in the name of individual freedom. They failed to see that government could be used for conservative ends.[17] Those we call liberals see the problem as an unfair system that rations advantages. They believe that government's role is to change the system so as to free poor people to pursue their interests just as others have. These liberals argued that the system did not provide enough jobs or jobs that were good enough or job training for good jobs or social services to help people take those jobs or training. Many liberals (such as Schorr) simply did not give the poor the credit of thinking they could make it on their own.[18] Economic theories stressed market incentives; labor unions feared competition from recipients required to work; the National Welfare Rights Organization claimed recipients had a right to an adequate income; organized religion claimed that people had a God-given worth that justified at least minimal support. What none of these liberals could bring themselves to advocate was the use of government authority in "a benevolent *and* direct way."[19] For Mead the problem finally goes back to John Locke's individualism, which permeates all of American political culture. Americans want to be left alone to pursue their own interests. "The idea of authoritative social programs supposes a more intimate involvement of government with the dependent, and vice versa, than most Americans can ever entirely accept."[20]

THE CIVIC CONCEPTION

Mead's alternative to this Lockean individualism is the civic conception. This civic conception prizes "the participation of all Americans in a common web of political and economic activity."[21] From this point of view, poverty (especially welfare poverty) is not a monetary problem so much as a problem of social exclusion. In American society the basis of membership in the mainstream for able-bodied people is economic independence—work. As long as welfare programs move people toward independence, they are consistent with this civic ideal. When they foster dependence, they are not. Within the welfare reform debates advocates, of the civic conception supported a work requirement in order to force recipients "to behave in integrating ways."[22]

Mead confronts the Lockean commitment to individual freedom even more directly:

> There is even a touch here of the classical idea that the citizen must in some senses be *un*free. He is not simply a natural man possessing rights carried over from the state of nature, as in Locke. He is also a civic man, the product of his own polity, and stamped by the rights *and* obligations that derive from it.[23]

Liberals assumed that America was rich enough to guarantee an income to all; conservatives believed the market provided plenty of opportunities for people to support themselves. The civic moderates wanted to guarantee income for those unable to work but to guarantee jobs for those able to work. For the employable, then, assistance is tied to the obligation that they work. The general public seems to share this contractual view of welfare, supporting benefits for those in need but demanding work of those who receive them.

For this civic conception of life, equality takes on a meaning different from that commonly assumed. Americans typically do not support economic equality in any absolute sense; they do not even care that much about social equality. What they do feel very strongly about is equal citizenship. Moreover, this form of equality "is not so much an entitlement, a status, as an *activity*."[24] Citizens work, pay taxes, and obey the law; they meet the obligations as well as claim the rights of citizenship and expect the same of others. To catch a sense of what Mead means here notice how often reference is made in public speeches to law-abiding citizens or average taxpayers. The public's desire to provide guaranteed employment to those who can work is moral more than mean:

> A substantial class of nonworking adults simply violates the American idea of equality. Those who function in the ways citizenship requires cannot feel equal to others who do not, when it seems they could. The stigma of welfare stems mainly from the frequent incompetence of the dependent, and the shame is felt by society as well as the recipients. The moral purpose of functioning requirements is to ensure, for their own benefit and others', that recipients do in fact discharge the common obligations of citizenship.[25]

When people discharge these obligations they are more fully integrated into the functioning mainstream. According to Mead, this is what Americans mean by equality.

Mead concludes by summarizing those obligations that typify the American mainstream and restating the need for authoritative government. He lists five basic social obligations for adults in the United States:

- Working if one is able,
- Supporting one's family as much as possible,
- Speaking and writing English,
- Learning enough to get a job, and
- Following the law.[26]

Consistent with Mead's whole approach, government assistance should be conditional upon the recipient meeting these obligations. In setting these standards, government is defining just what citizenship means. Failure to set such standards weakens the meaning of citizenship for all of us. To do this, government must recognize its responsibility not just to extend individual freedom but also to impose and preserve social obligation. For Mead, we must move beyond entitlement to responsibility if our society is to hold together. This brings us to our five moral questions.

INDIVIDUALITY

When we begin to compare Mead with Murray and Schorr in terms of how they respond to the five ethical questions we have posed, we must first note a shift of focus away from the individual. Most Americans share a set of expectations about what people should do, which centers upon self-determination. However, Mead is clear that we are not born with these expectations but rather learn them from the society of which we are a part. Nevertheless, he places the primary responsibility for developing that self-determination in the hands of the individual. Any attempt to transfer that responsibility to the government, such as what Schorr proposes, treats the client paternalistically. Instead, he proposes a social contract that clearly expects (or even demands) self-determination from people. Liberal critics would say that he blames the victim of social disadvantage. He claims that he is holding them responsible and thus refusing to treat them like victims.

Mead's recognition of society's role in shaping individuals keeps him from adopting Murray's approach of leaving individuals alone to make their way in the world. These rules of behavior are society's rules, and it is up to government to support them and those individuals who seek to live by them. He rejects Murray's rugged individualism in favor of social integration. Indeed, he continually complains that the American tradition is far too individualistic. For example, he complains about both liberals and conservatives: "The thread that connects them is trust in the individual at the expense of authority, a desire to make the realization of his or her desires the basis of social order."[27] He believes that we live a social conformity necessary to the stability of our society without ever having recognized it in our political ideas. In simple terms, nearly all of us learned from society to expect to work and to support our families, and we expect our fellow citizens to do the same. That is what holds our society together. Mead fears social chaos much more than he does loss of personal freedom.

COMMUNITY

So Mead stresses community, but of what sort? Perhaps the key to understanding Mead's conception of community is to recognize that he believes that our society basically works. It is based on certain shared values of work and family and law which it teaches its citizens. Our society depends upon its citizens holding dear these values and acting upon them. Mead believes these basic shared values are good and that the social and economic system fairly rewards those people who live by those values. He seeks an ordered society where individuals conform to the basic values of society. Moreover, he is willing to force people to conform, quoting Hobbes on the need for obedience to authority under any political system. He concludes: "Community has indeed dissolved in the low-wage labor market. For it to be restored, work must apparently become a duty for the least skilled, not just a matter of self-interest."[28] Social integration is more important than individual rights, and self-interest cannot be trusted to pull the community together.

In the long run, however, Mead is convinced that this conformity to society's values will be good for the individual also. Policies that require such things as work do limit freedom, but this is more than justified by their contribution to social order. However, Mead goes on to claim:

> A sense of personal obligation is in fact necessary to freedom. Parents teach their children to be "responsible," that is, to obey reasonable requirements levied by others and to be accountable for their behavior. Individuals must be *un*free in these senses in order to live independent lives.[29]

It is important to note that Mead expresses openly here the paternalism that pervades his whole analysis. Poor people are like irresponsible children, and government must be their parents. In order to be independent and self-determining, adults must learn to follow society's rules. So it is good for people if government, as the representative of society, forces them to be responsible.

WORTH

It seems clear that for Mead a person's worth is defined by society's basic shared values. Persons who do not live up to those values are problems that must be brought back into conformity. The problem is not an unjust society but rather people who have failed to function in ways generally expected by society. His goal is to get people who are not functioning by America's values to internalize those values and act upon them. As he puts it, "Far from blaming people if they deviate, government must persuade them to *blame themselves.*"[30] There is here none of Schorr's nearly unlimited affirmation of the inherent value of each person. This is understandable for someone of Murray's persuasion who assumes that individuals are the final reality, and therefore each of us must justify ourselves by earning our place in the world.

Mead's rejection of the inherent worth of people is a bit more confusing. He believes that society teaches us our basic values. If so, why is it not at least in part society's fault when someone has not learned what society has taught? Mead's answer seems to be that society does bear some responsibility and must exercise it by requiring people to live by those shared values. What he never talks about is whether the social and economic system genuinely allows people a realistic possibility of living by those values. Are jobs available for poor people to go to work and support their families, or are schools available that provide poor children with a real possibility of gaining the education necessary to succeed? Mead seems merely to assume so. In any event, he certainly does not share the view that we shall see in Piven that society does not provide real opportunity to poor people and that society must change. The most important thing government must do is not to provide support for those in need but rather to reinforce the obligation of the poor to behave as mainstream society expects.

MOTIVATION

Murray and his cohorts believe people are motivated simply by self-interest and that incentives should be set up so that it is in people's self-interest to work. Mead believes it may well be impossible to create incentives sufficient to get people on welfare to take the dirty, low-paying jobs available to them. In part, this is because Mead simply does not believe that the general population wants to eliminate public welfare totally as Murray proposes. Therefore, since society has a great stake in people working, it should require them to do so. He also seems to believe that once people have learned the value of work, that value will motivate them as much as self-interest. However, Mead does not share Schorr's belief in positive motivation. If Schorr is the forever-supportive parent, Mead believes in tough love. To do better, poor people who do not practice mainstream values must be punished, not just offered support.

Mead does not share Murray's view that aid to the poor should be cut back dramatically. Rather, he believes that the vast majority of Americans are more than willing to pay taxes to help the poor, if the poor behave properly. He constantly argues that the issue is not money, not the immediate individual self-interest of the taxpayers. Rather, the issue at the core of the welfare debate is moral and social. Society has certain shared values in which the vast majority of citizens must believe or the society will fall apart. The poor must practice these values just like everyone else. Moreover, society must not be seen as tolerating anything less or the values will become less binding on everyone. For Mead, social obligation must be seen as at least equal to self-interest as a motivating factor for humans.

HOPE

As already suggested, Mead neither expects nor advocates significant change in the overall society, at least not positive ones. If anything, he fears change, especially the weakening of the traditional values of mainstream America. In this sense he is profoundly conservative, seeking to conserve the values of the past and preserve and strengthen them. Mead also sees no need to change social and economic realities to square with these traditional values. For instance, instead of proposing a significant program of job creation or job upgrading, he supports requiring people to work at the jobs that are presently available. In fact, he believes that recipients' complaints about the kind of jobs available or the inadequacy of job training or child care are usually just excuses people use to get out of their social obligations. Mead's hope is not to change society but rather to enforce conformity to society's present values.

Mead's analysis has become increasingly persuasive to many Americans, replacing Murray's as the standard source of conservative criticisms of welfare and proposals to reform it. At the same time, more liberal appeals for social integration—such as those of Daniel Patrick Moynihan, which we shall take up later—have become more popular. Finally, more radical communitarian visions, many from religious sources, continue to gain adherents. The growing popularity of these communitarian views, especially among conservatives, flows from the general anxiety that our society is verging on chaos. This is the real emotional core of the religious right and of so-called neoconservatives. While conservatives still talk often about the free market, most Americans are much more concerned that their kids are out of control, the work ethic is weakening, and the traditional family is falling apart. It is this fear of coming anarchy to which Mead appeals so profoundly. For those who feel this fear, it is about time someone like Mead spoke up for social order instead of individual freedom or social change.

CONCLUSION

Lawrence Mead revives the traditional conservative defense of social order. He believes that the community must establish and enforce certain values basic to that social order—like work and family. This need for social order must override the short-term desires of individuals in order to make them productive participants in the society in the long run. For Mead, human worth is earned by living up to society's standards. Self-interest is not a dependable measure of the importance of social order. He neither desires nor expects much fundamental change. Drawing upon this basic view of the world, Mead describes poverty as a failure of social authority, leading to dependency rather than self-sufficiency. Thus, welfare policy must enforce the basic values of work and family as the price recipients pay for assistance.

CHAPTER SEVEN

STRUGGLING AGAINST AN UNJUST SYSTEM: FRANCES FOX PIVEN

When Lloyd Ohlin set out for Washington to attempt to put his theory to work for the President's Committee on Juvenile Delinquency and Crime and then the War on Poverty,[1] his colleague Richard Cloward began to work more closely with Frances Fox Piven. Together they analyzed and defended the Mobilization for Youth program, publicized and supported the National Welfare Rights Organization, and wrote a seminal work on United States welfare policy—*Regulating the Poor*.[2] Throughout, their position has been a consistent advocacy of the right of the poor to a greater return from the capitalist system and of the need to disrupt that system until it responds. Increasingly, Piven has taken on this role of welfare rights advocate on her own, so we shall focus on her in our analysis although much of her published work has been as a joint author with Cloward. Put simply, Frances Fox Piven has been the strongest advocate for the poor in welfare policy debates for three decades.

The central conviction in Piven's analysis is that poverty is a failure of the economic, political, and social system, not the fault of the poor. In fact, she argues that the economic system dominates our political and social life, and its demands explain the place of poverty in particular in our society. As she sees it, capitalists need a pool of cheap labor so they can maximize their profits. If government acts to end poverty, by providing either jobs or income, people will not have to work for low wages. For capitalists, then, the ideal policy would be no assistance for the poor. However, capitalists and especially politicians also want a calm society in which business as usual can go on. As a result, the greatest power that the poor have is the capacity to disrupt the social peace, to cause trouble.

PIVEN'S HISTORY OF WELFARE

Piven describes the basic rhythm of welfare policy as follows: Welfare benefits are low to force people to work, the poor disrupt society, politicians act to bring peace by increasing benefits for the poor, the poor quiet down, and then benefits are cut in order to restore the low-wage labor pool.[3] Notice that she does not expect anyone in this whole process to act out of the goodness of his or her heart. So it is that Piven's story of previous eras of reform emphasizes the place of public demonstrations and civil disruptions. The Progressives were responding to marches by workers; Franklin Roosevelt shifted his policies in a more liberal direction because the poor were in the streets and threatening to vote for someone more radical.[4]

In telling the story of the explosion of the welfare rolls in the late sixties, she begins with the shift in the means of agricultural production (especially in the South) by the introduction of machines to replace farm workers.[5] Agricultural states, again especially in the South, refused to provide benefits to the workers who lost their jobs. So it was a combination of a major economic shift *and* the failure of government to respond to the human impact of that shift that pushed people out of the agricultural South. This push was reinforced by the pull of industrial jobs in cities, especially in the North, leading to the great migration of poor, mostly black, Southern agricultural workers from farm to city.

In 1910, three-fourths of African Americans lived in agricultural areas and nine-tenths in the South; by 1960, three-fourths of African Americans lived in cities and one-half in the North. Whites, especially poor ones, migrated in similar directions if in smaller proportions. When the migrants arrived in the cities they found fewer jobs and more unemployment than they expected. They also found tough welfare laws and administrators, so they did not go on welfare in great numbers. Only after the demonstrations and disruptions of the sixties did politicians relax welfare law and regulations in order to restore peace, leading to an explosion in the welfare rolls.[6] Basic economic changes set the scene, but only social disorder (or at least the threat of it) forced the political issue, producing more money for the poor. Since then, the poor have become quiet, benefits have been cut, and demands for more cuts abound.

Piven's specific interpretation of what happened in the sixties and seventies is very much at odds with the others we have seen. It is very much the account of the political effect of social movements. First, she dismisses some of the specific explanations popularly believed. For instance, she points out that most of the migration was in the forties and fifties, but the welfare rolls did not expand. People did not move to get on welfare. Similarly, benefit levels went up more in the fifties than in the sixties but welfare rolls did not go up very much. People did not go on welfare just because benefits increased. She also challenges the view that family change is a major cause of welfare expansion, contending that studies indicate that only 10 percent of the increase in welfare between 1959 and 1966 can be attributed to family changes.[7]

Rather than any of these three factors, Piven roots the explanation of welfare expansion in the economic reality of a series of recessions during the decade after the Korean War. This produced particularly high unemployment rates among the poor, especially for the young and black. This high unemployment in turn caused social disorder— gangs, delinquency, drug trade, crime, and family breakup—and a growing weakening of respect for symbols of authority such as police, firefighters, and politicians. It is hard to remember she is describing the early sixties not the early nineties.

THE GREAT SOCIETY

None of this was of political import yet. Several forces joined to convert economic changes and social problems into political forces. The Civil Rights Movement challenged racial segregation, primarily to the benefit of middle-class blacks. The hopes of the black masses were raised but with little result, leading to calls for black empowerment. Businesses, especially large ones, no longer saw much profit to be gained from racism and were afraid of social disorder. The religious and philanthropic elite increasingly supported the claims of the urban poor and emphasized self-determination. Finally, the black vote had grown to a size that required Northern political leaders to take it much more seriously.[8] So, when civil disturbances spread across American cities between 1964 and 1968, politicians at both the local and national levels sought to restore civil peace by increasing benefits to the poor. Notice that while Piven's description takes account of the contribution of elites, the primary actors that force changes are the masses in revolt.

Piven suggests that the federal antipoverty effort can be broadly understood as the attempt of the Democratic Party to cope with the electoral significance of the great migration once civil disorder appeared.[9] This federal effort led specifically to the rapid expansion of welfare rolls through three related developments. As antipoverty offices opened in poor communities across the country, one main service they provided was help in getting on welfare and getting all of the benefits possible. Second, an integral part of the War on Poverty was legal services for the poor. These poverty lawyers quickly realized that one way they could help the poor was to bring class action suits to challenge various welfare regulations for a whole group of people rather than just for an individual. They did; they were often successful; and the welfare rolls grew. Finally, one of the stated goals of Community Action within the War on Poverty was to help the poor get organized. One natural group for organization was welfare recipients. The resulting National Welfare Rights Organization (NWRO) not only advocated more generous assistance but also helped poor people get on welfare and know about all of the benefits that were available to them.[10]

Just as the Civil Rights Movement was increasingly replaced by the Black Power Movement, the most militant advocates came to power in the Community Action Agencies and especially in the NWRO. They disrupted political meetings, embarrassed and criticized public officials, demonstrated against things they did not like, and generally caused trouble. This led politicians to look for ways to tame these militants by setting up political and legal limits on their power and by expanding welfare programs to buy off the masses of the poor. Generally they succeeded in restoring social and political peace. Notice that in Piven's account it is not some soft-hearted liberal elite convinced of a new theory of poverty that creates an expansion of welfare as Murray contends. Rather, it is pragmatic capitalists and their political servants acting to restore the social peace necessary to the survival of the capitalist system by buying off the disruptive poor masses.

Piven pulls together all of the elements of this description of the welfare explosion in the following words:

> In summary, modernization, migration, urban unemployment, the breakup of families, rising grant levels, and other factors contributed to a growing pool of "eligible" families in the 1950s and 1960s. Nevertheless, the relief rolls did not rise until the 1960s. And when they did, it was largely as a result of governmental programs designed to moderate widespread political unrest among the black poor. One consequence of these programs was that the poor were suddenly stimulated to apply for relief in unprecedented numbers (except in the South); another consequence was that welfare officials were suddenly stimulated to approve applications in unprecedented numbers. The result was the relief explosion of the late 1960s. The terms in which that crisis must be explained are economic disruption, large-scale migration, mass volatility, and electoral responses—a sequence of disturbances leading to a precipitous expansion of the relief rolls.[11]

Her conclusion from all that she has described can be stated simply, "the moral seems clear: a placid poor get nothing, but a turbulent poor sometimes get something."[12]

PIVEN'S POLICY PROPOSALS

Piven is very ambiguous about policy recommendations. She and Cloward argued for basic economic reforms "that would lead to full employment at decent wages" at the end of *Regulating the Poor*.[13] Full employment would both help the working poor directly and reduce the pressure on welfare by allowing many of the welfare poor to go to work. Yet she was doubtful that would happen. In the absence of such basic economic change, she feared that welfare reform would simply be an excuse to take money away from the poor and make them work at bad jobs. She strongly supported the welfare reform proposals of the National Welfare Rights Organization, which called for a minimum national benefit equivalent to the Lower Living Standard Budget of Bureau of Labor Statistics. That was about $5,500 for a family of four in 1968 and would be about $22,000 in 1993, if they still published it. Like full employment this proposal has also never been a real political possibility. Rather, various welfare reform proposals were aimed at forcing the poor to work at low wages. Given the unlikeliness of either a full employment economy or a general reform of welfare, Piven and Cloward concluded, "In the absence of fundamental economic reforms, therefore, *we take the position that the explosion of the rolls is the true relief reform,* that it should be defended, and expanded."[14]

By 1984, Piven was somewhat less enthusiastic about full employment because of an increasing awareness of the convergence of poverty and gender. She argues that full employment is a strategy that addresses male poverty better than female poverty.[15] Traditionally, men have not been as able as women to qualify for welfare. At the same time, women's jobs have traditionally paid much less than have men's. Moreover, she argues that the real earnings of the jobs that women tend to hold has declined in recent years. So, while a few well-prepared women have been able to move into well-paying jobs usually held by men, most women are left behind in jobs held mostly by women and not paying enough to support a family. Women, then, have a particular stake in welfare. Women constitute a large proportion of welfare recipients, working women need welfare in order to be able to risk being fired when they try to improve their situation, and 70 percent of the jobs administering welfare are held by women. For all of these reasons, Piven urges women's organizations to join the battle to defend welfare as essential to the economic survival of many women.[16]

It is not at all incidental to Piven's analysis that organizations of the poor have disappeared. The fact that women's organizations exist and are sensitive to the charge that they essentially are middle class is part of the reason why she seeks to show that welfare is a women's issue. Piven is always looking for a social movement with enough power to protect welfare benefits from attack from business interests. For Piven, the absence of organized groups of the poor or significant disruption by the poor also explains why welfare is presently under challenge from all sides. This fits neatly within her overall thesis that the ebb and flow of welfare benefits depends upon how quiet the poor are. Since the poor are now mostly quiet and disorganized, welfare advocates like Piven are on the defensive, trying as best she can to minimize the losses until the next period of activism and expansion. Part of Piven's immediate task, then, is to respond to such critics of welfare as Murray and Mead.[17]

PIVEN'S RESPONSE TO MURRAY AND MEAD

Perhaps the key to understanding Piven's position is to recognize that she views scholarship as advocacy. She is clear that she is an advocate for the interests of the poor. She assumes that the perspective of the poor, especially the activist poor, on welfare is basically true. This becomes central to Piven's criticism of Murray and Mead because she challenges their claims of objectivity. Rather, she is convinced that they are advocates for business interests, whether they realize it or not. As we have seen, welfare creates problems for business. Workers have welfare as an alternative to low-wage work, which allows them to refuse to work at those wages or under conditions they do not like. This is true even for workers who are not themselves eligible for welfare, because employers have a harder time finding workers to replace them. Murray and Mead, she says, criticize the same benefits as work disincentives, meaning they are bad for business.[18]

Essential to the political success of the pro-business attack on welfare is to convince the majority of workers that welfare is against their interests and even destructive of the poor in the long run. She calls those assertions the "Great Relief Hoax" because they contradict what might otherwise be obvious, "that people whose labor is of little value in the market are better off when they receive income protections, and that most other workers are also better off when they no longer have to compete with such vulnerable workers."[19] The first of the false assertions by Murray is that welfare somehow hurts those poor who work when it actually strengthens their bargaining position. The second is that if welfare were eliminated the former recipients would go to work. In fact, Piven argues that studies indicate that the primary result would be 5 to 7 percent increase in unemployment. The final false assertion is that welfare creates problems in the recipients, specifically a lack of motivation for work and a weakening of the family unit. In fact, Piven believes the poor do take on some deviant behavior, but that is because they are poor, not because of welfare. In the case of motivation to work, Piven points out that most recipients move into jobs when they are available in times of economic growth.

In the case of family life, Piven takes particular pains to respond to Murray. She argues that migration from farm to city and long years of poverty and unemployment have led to a deterioration of the traditional poor family, especially among African Americans. These results were apparent long before the increase in welfare in the late

109

sixties. However, women and children generally were taken in by other family members and so were not counted by the census as a separate household. AFDC did allow many of these women to establish a separate household and thus be counted as a single-parent family by the census. According to Piven, welfare did not cause family breakup; it only caused us to notice it. She concludes:

> To sum up, migration and urban unemployment and subemployment put the black family under intense stress after 1940, and the proportion of single-parent families began to climb. The full extent of this growth was not recorded officially, however, until a pattern of independent living was set in motion by mass protest and the rise of welfare rolls that followed in the late 1960s. In other words, *single-parent families were much less likely to be counted before the AFDC rolls expanded, and they were much more likely to be counted thereafter.*[20]

To force such women back into traditional families with men who are unemployed unless jobs at adequate wages are available will not end poverty and may result in more domestic violence and child abuse.

In the final analysis, then, the issue for Piven is whether people are to be left to the insecurities of the market or are to be provided with some measure of security by the government. Clearly Murray prefers the market alone; Mead wants government to act to reinforce the market. Piven agrees with them that welfare does reduce the incentive to work for low wages in bad working conditions. However, she sees this as an achievement, not a failing. She concludes:

> The income supports that reduce insecurity and make people more independent also blunt the force of market incentives and disincentives. After all, desperate people without any protections at all will work at any job, no matter how harsh the terms. This is at the heart of what the conflict over the welfare state is about, and it is what conflicts over relief have always been about.[21]

Piven charges that Murray and Mead have taken their stand with the business interests while she stands with the workers, including the poor. This brings us to our ethical questions.

INDIVIDUALITY

Among the four positions we have considered, Piven emphasizes most the limits society places upon our individual self-determination.

At every turn she argues that large social forces and the dynamics of the market economy rather than individual choices are the causes of human behavior. In particular, the poor adjust and cope with these larger forces, and the suggestion that they control their own destiny is part of the hoax apologists for business interests try to put over on us to keep us from seeing the limits of the market system. In this, she differs most clearly and directly from Murray, who wants to leave individuals entirely on their own to succeed or fail in the market. From her point of view, Mead's advocacy of the community is flawed by his defense of the status quo and willingness to force people to conform to mainstream values rather than recognizing that those values reinforce the interests of business. Finally, Schorr simply fails to come to terms with the need to change the basic social and economic system.

Lacking opportunity, poor people cope in part by behaving in deviant ways. However, Piven does not agree that this represents fundamental damage to the human spirit or the guiding values of the poor. Rather, when real opportunity is available, the poor act just like everyone else in order to achieve the same basic goals as the rest of us. The poor do not need a values conversion; they need an economic and social system that allows them to achieve the same values as the rest of society. Short of such social change, the poor and their allies find themselves in a struggle. Fighting the system is an affirmation of self-worth as well as a strategy for forcing the system to deliver more benefits to the poor.

COMMUNITY

This helps us begin to understand Piven's view of community. In many ways, she shares Mead's view that government's role is to reinforce the system. The difference, of course, is that Mead sees this as a solution while Piven struggles against it. Government seeks to incorporate disparate groups into the mainstream especially if they are threatening the social peace. At least under the capitalist system, social peace is the enemy of the poor, according to Piven. Conflict and struggle are essential if the community is to take seriously the needs of the poor. A smoothly operating, peaceful capitalist society masks the day-to-day struggle of those at the bottom to survive on low wages and poor working conditions or little income at all. She would suspect strongly that Mead's advocacy of a well-integrated community masks the denial of the just interests of the poor.

This returns us to the question of self-determination. Individual poor persons acting alone are not likely to change society very much, but people joining together in movements can force the established powers to act. In a real sense, the poor must realize their community of shared interest and join together to express it in uncompromising terms. Inasmuch as possible the movements of the poor must find other communities—women, low-wage workers, and so on—to join with in broader movements. However, these movements must remain clear that there are enemies out there, powerful business interests, who will fight them at every turn. Getting sucked into a concern for the whole community only tends to weaken the resolve necessary to make the strongest possible case for those without power. Piven advises the poor to be suspicious of those who call for peace and instead to use the establishment's desire for peace to get rewards from it.[22]

WORTH

Schorr challenges Murray and Mead on the issue of human worth, offering endless grace, but she retains an emphasis on the individual. Piven advocates both grace and social change and thus challenges the common wisdom upon which both Murray and Mead base their positions. Perhaps this is illustrated most clearly by the welfare reform proposal advocated by the National Welfare Rights Organization, which Piven supported from beginning to end. The NWRO proposed a minimum national benefit at the level of the Bureau of Labor Statistics Lower Living Budget, about $22,000 in today's dollars *as a right*. *As a right* was stressed over and over again to affirm intentionally the basic worth of every human, whether or not he or she was successful in generally accepted terms. No one feature of the proposal drew more fire from conservative critics than this audacious statement of the worth of the poor.

This basic affirmation is fundamental to Piven's position. The poor are just as valuable as anyone else but are victims of an unjust society. Society, or more particularly the business elite who benefit from the capitalist system, is to blame for poverty, not the poor. The poor affirm their worth by joining in movements to fight that system and those

who are not poor recognize the true worth of human life by supporting those movements. Obviously, Piven did just this herself by supporting, publicizing, and lending legitimacy to the National Welfare
Rights Organization.[23] For Piven, the poor are worth just as much as
the rest of us and deserve a bigger piece of the economic pie than
they are getting. How that pie is cut is a matter of interests and power,
not what people have legitimately earned. The poor and their supporters must challenge those in power in part by undermining their
claim that they deserve more because they have worked for it. The
poor must demand their *rightful* piece of the pie.

MOTIVATION

Piven is pretty cynical about human nature. Business interests, which
she identifies as the essential opponents of the poor, support the market
system because it makes them rich and powerful. When politicians
respond to the needs of the poor it is because they want to restore social
peace so they can stay in office. The poor themselves need to assert their
self-interest in the strongest possible terms, and workers need to recognize that their self-interest lies with the poor, not with business interests.
She tries to unmask the claim of objectivity by Murray and Mead, whom
she considers mere apologists for business interests. She is even skeptical
of soft-hearted social-work types like Schorr. To advocate social services
ahead of money for the poor is to substitute the self-interests of middle-
class professionals (teachers, social workers, and medical personnel) for
the self-interests of the poor. It would be much more honest to advocate
social services in the interest of the women who are the majority of those
professionals (as she does).[24]

Positive change is much more likely to occur when we fully recognize the interests at work in our debate over welfare policy, not from
selfless sacrifice by anyone. Piven finally supports the demand of the poor
not because the poor do not have self-interest but because their self-
interest has been served so poorly by the capitalists. In a sense, she seeks
less a world where we will all share out of the goodness of our hearts than
one where the poor will have a greater chance to achieve their interests,
just as the rich and the powerful do now. Much of this analysis of human
nature flows from Piven's basically Marxist analysis of capitalism. The
difference is that she expects no revolution in the United States any time

soon, and therefore does not talk of a new communal humanity after that revolution as does Marx. For Piven, we are all basically self-interested, and the only hope is that those whose interests are served poorly now will demand more from the system.

One matter of human nature that Piven constantly presses is that the powerful can be best motivated by threatening them. This leads to her stress on conflict and disorder as the primary means of getting more for the poor. Her critics would question this analysis in principle as well as in practice.[25] Psychologists suggest that people generally respond better to reward than to punishment, and Piven herself suggests that poor people are more likely to respond to positive incentives than to punishing restrictions. Why not assume similarly that the rich and powerful are more likely to respond positively to positive possibilities than negative threats? For instance, will not the hope that by reducing poverty our work force and economy will be more productive and all of us better off move more people than the threat that if we do not deal with poverty the poor will burn the country down? This question can be raised much more specifically in relation to Piven's history of the sixties. Did the War on Poverty arise out of civil disorders, or did it arise before the major disorders out of the hopes raised by the Kennedy and early Johnson eras? Indeed, it can be argued that the civil disorders of the mid to late sixties led to a law-and-order president, Richard Nixon, who cut assistance to the poor and shifted money into law-and-order programs. Piven disagrees, arguing consistently that those with money and power only give it up when faced with direct and honest threats.

HOPE

This brings us to the question of hope. Because Piven does not expect human nature to change, those with power will fight to keep it. Those without power in capitalist societies are disorganized and on the defensive. Even when they have been organized and aggressive they have only been able to increase their piece of the benefits of the system a little bit. What she describes is a sort of endless ebb and flow within the capitalist system. The poor cause trouble, and they get some new benefits; they quiet down, and the benefits are withdrawn. The system, however, does not change. The more clearly Piven draws the irresolvable conflict in interests between the rich and powerful and the poor, the more starkly she describes the power of the rich and the disorganization of the poor, the less likely change seems.

In the current situation, Piven argues that what is finally at stake in our debate over welfare policy is the market and the traditional family.[26] She is clear that the needs of the poor and low-wage workers take precedence over the needs of the market and that the traditional family masks male domination and violence. Thus, the issues at stake are very profound.[27] Yet, perhaps precisely because the issues cut so deeply and because it is so difficult to articulate a common interest that is not equivalent to the interests of those in power, she offers little hope of change at a level deep enough to affect these fundamental issues. The best that those without power and money can hope for is a few more crumbs off the table if they shake it enough.

CONCLUSION

Frances Fox Piven has been a consistent advocate of fundamental change in American society as the only real solution for domestic poverty. Her basic principle is that communities shape individuals, for good or ill. To her, the poor are innocent victims of an unjust society; given the opportunity the poor will act like everyone else; all people are motivated primarily by self-interest; and there is not much chance that the necessary social changes will happen. Consistent with these principles, Piven believes poverty is a necessary by-product of the capitalist system. Until that capitalist system is changed dramatically, she urges the poor and their supporters to try to get just as much welfare as they can.

CHAPTER EIGHT

WORLD VIEWS, THEOLOGIES, AND SOCIAL ETHICS

As Charles Murray describes the life of his mythical couple Harold and Phyllis, the choice between welfare and work is key. Back in 1960 before welfare became generous, work was Harold's only real option. "It is not much of a living, not much of a job. There is no future in it, no career path. But it pays for food and shelter. And Harold has no choice."[1] For Murray, those were the good old days. Piven agrees with his description of the relation between welfare and low-wage work. "The income supports that reduce insecurity and make people more independent also blunt the force of market incentives and disincentives. After all, desperate people without any protections at all will work at any job no matter how harsh the terms."[2] For Murray this represents the most obvious danger of welfare benefits; for Piven, "that is their great accomplishment."[3] Thus, Murray concludes that welfare must be eliminated so it does not compete with marginal jobs. To the contrary, Piven concludes that welfare benefits must be protected and expanded in order to increase the power of the poor, both those on welfare and those who work.

How can Murray and Piven see the same reality so differently? The answer, of course, is that their views of the world are so different because they begin from very different places in that world. Murray stands in the midst of a market system, which he believes functions efficiently and moreover fairly rewards honest effort on the part of individuals. Piven stands with the poor whom she believes have not been treated fairly by the very system that Murray reveres. From their two very different vantage points, they see welfare programs and almost everything else from what seem like diametrically opposed angles. Perspective makes all the difference. For social ethics the essential religious insight is that some particular state of affairs is unjust. Our basic theological task is to choose a view of the world from which this injustice can be seen clearly and to give reasons for this choice.

THE FOUR PERSPECTIVES

Let us return to the four alternatives we have before us and then turn to that theological task. Usually it is helpful to use a comparative framework for comparing and contrasting fundamentally different ways of looking at something. We are now in a position to place these four analyses of poverty and welfare within such a framework in much more specific terms. In the Western tradition, the classic framework for such comparison is the four causes identified by Aristotle.[4] The point is not that each position deals with only one of Aristotle's four causes but that each emphasizes one of the various aspects of causation identified by Aristotle.

Charles Murray believes that the fundamental reality is the choosing individual. In Aristotelian language this choosing individual is the *efficient* cause of human action. Social institutions and cultural patterns are but the results of choices that individuals make, including the choice to cooperate with others on something. Wealth and poverty are the results of choices individuals have made—wise or foolish, greedy or sacrificial. For Murray, providing the grounds for these individual choices is the proper place for religion. At the same time, Murray believes that public policy should leave people free to decide without government intervention.

Lisbeth Schorr also begins with individuals and families, but she believes that intervention can help these individuals make much better choices. In Aristotelian language, the character of these individuals is the *material* cause of human action. This belief is fueled by some general ideal of a healthy and competent person. Poor people make poor choices because they do not have the necessary personal or financial resources. With support from a wide range of social services most disadvantaged people can make their way in the world, and as a result all of us will be much better for it. Thus, public policy should aim at providing the help necessary for poor people to develop the personal strength to pull their lives together.

Lawrence Mead argues that contemporary conservatives and liberals alike are afraid to exercise the authority that government must use to establish and maintain social order. In Aristotelian language, this social order is the *formal* cause of human action. Conservatives like Murray seek to minimize government, including assistance to the poor, in the name of expanding individual freedom. Because liberals like Schorr blame society for the problems of deviant behavior, they advocate government-financed services to support the poor rather than enforcing standards for their behavior. Mead contends that society must establish such basic standards of acceptable behavior, the most important in the case of poverty being the requirement that people work. These standards of behavior are essential to the basic order necessary to the survival of a society, and society should expect and require individuals to fulfill that responsibility to society. Furthering social order is the first priority of government.

Throughout her participation in the struggle over poverty and welfare, *Frances Fox Piven has argued for a good society that provides good jobs or adequate income for all.* In Aristotelian language, this just society is the *final* cause of human action. Like all the other public issues, for her the causes of poverty are social, and the solutions must be structural. Humans are essentially communal, shaped for ill or good by the character of the community. Only social changes that reshape the very structure of our economy so that it provides good jobs to all of those who want to work really will address poverty fully. Failing that, the poor and their supporters should try to get as much of the pie as possible. The community she imagines is inclusive and diverse, marked by continual coalition building, conflict, and democratic debate. The one she sees is dominated by an elite that controls the economy for its own interests unless challenged by those out of power.

Another way of summarizing the differences among these four perspectives is to recognize that two of the four stress the individual (Murray and Schorr) and two stress the community (Mead and Piven). They can then be further distinguished by the fact that two (Murray and Mead) pretty much accept the reality they stress, the individual or the community, as it is.[5] The other two (Schorr and Piven) argue for changing the reality they stress, the individual or the community, toward some ideal. These distinctions can be expressed in the following way:

	Phenomenal	Ontic
Individual	Murray	Schorr
Community	Mead	Piven

The term *phenomenal* refers to the fact that Murray advocates individual choice but offers no standard for judging which choices are good except that they lead to success in the market. Similarly, Mead advocates social stability but offers no standards for determining what is a good society. On the other hand, *ontic* refers to the fact that Schorr has a normative view of what a mature person should be like and wants to provide the supportive services necessary to help the poor develop in that way. Similarly, Piven has a general concept of what would make a community just.

While this structure may well finally be based in the same basic differences as the traditional four causes, I believe it helps us to understand the differences among the four welfare analyses much more clearly. Whether we play the traditional game of Aristotle's four causes or use this alternative structure, the basic point is the same. These are not just four interesting and influential authors on poverty and welfare, although that they are. They also represent four fundamentally different ways of looking at the world. We shall return to the meaning of these differences after I have developed my own basic world view.

WORLD VIEWS AND ETHICS

It is important to recognize that a person's view of the world organizes and shapes how that person thinks about ethical questions. That seems obvious enough. However, it becomes real only as it is made specific. So, let us take the time to remind ourselves just how the world views of our four authors lead to the answers they give to the five ethical questions we have asked.

Murray's central commitment to the choosing individual colors his view of other ethical issues. Since the community at its best is but a collection of independent individuals, the community should just stay out of the way of able-bodied adults. There is not much grace in the world as he sees it. We may be the recipient of generous or even sacrificial deeds from time to time, but fundamentally it is up to us to make our own way in the world. We succeed or fail by our choices. While he praises generous and even sacrificial acts if freely chosen, he assumes that most people most of the time will choose to advance their own interests. This is what makes a market economy efficient. Finally, Murray expects no dramatic changes in the way the world works, especially for poor people. The best he expects for his fictional characters Harold and Phyllis is for Harold to work away at a low-paying job, struggling to support his Phyllis and their children. In the final analysis, it is much better to fall on the downside of the market than to lose the freedom to choose.

Schorr's central commitment to the need to help the individual improve, influences Schorr's other ethical views. Like Murray the community is for her a collection of individuals, but better individuals make for a better community. Thus, the community should help develop individuals able to take care of themselves. For her, people are rich or poor primarily because of the accident of birth. Thus, people and especially children deserve help regardless of what they have or have not done. Murray expects good works from the poor; Schorr offers nearly limitless grace. Given proper support, Schorr expects people to improve. Indeed, the basic problem of the typical poor person is not greed but a weak self-image. She even believes that the nonpoor will support funding for these social service programs when we see that they help people. Cementing her standing as a naive liberal, Schorr concludes that the solutions to poverty and related social ills are quite within our reach, if we but generalize upon those social service programs that are already successfully addressing these ills.

Mead's emphasis on social order suggests that all individuals cannot be expected to be self-determining on their own and that society must be prepared to require individuals to behave in the normal way. Mead expects people to earn the right to be accepted into society by living up to these standards of behavior. For instance, government should practice very tough love, not grace, toward those who do not work. Permissiveness fails precisely because people will not work at unpleasant jobs unless they are required to do so. In contrast to Schorr's view that the poor need help in developing a more positive self-concept, Mead believes the poor will do as little as they can. Clearly, social order, not social change, is Mead's central concern. In fact, he portrays social change as disintegration to be feared and resisted. His central goal is to reinforce the present social order.

The community Piven seeks requires individuals who are assertive and competent, but who see their destiny tied to others to whom they are related in a wide variety of ways. For her, people are born into membership in the community. It is the responsibility of society to provide the support necessary for human development, not of the individual to earn that support. Unlike Schorr who shares this graceful view with her, Piven believes structural change, not social services to individuals, is the grace needed. Piven recognizes that poverty, and especially the irrational welfare system, may have produced people who behave in ways destructive to themselves and others. Her solution is to change the system so that it supports human development and human cooperation. This will happen, if at all, only as poor people and their allies cause the power structure enough trouble to force them to make the necessary social changes. While she is doubtful that the needed revolution is likely any time soon, she sees no other hope.

WORLD VIEWS AND THEOLOGIES

If, as I suggested, the choice of a world view from which justice can be perceived is the most important theological task for social ethics, we should expect each of the four alternative world views we have examined to have theologies associated with them. They do.

Charles Murray's world view has been the dominant one in American history. At least since Max Weber's time it has been associated with the Protestant work ethic.[6] Its American roots are usually traced back to the New England Puritans. In fact, those Puritans stressed community much more than Weber suggested.[7] American individualism finds its truest advocates in the exiles from, or the opponents to, the Puritans—the free churches. Baptists and Methodists were the true entrepreneurs of American religion.[8] Reinforced later by the secular faiths in market competition and survival of the fittest, it is this tradition of rugged individualism that became the dominant theology of America.[9] It remains so.

Now its loudest advocates are the new evangelicals, who often tie individual salvation and economic success together.[10] They usually get their inspiration from scriptural references to our direct relation to God. America likes nothing better than the story of a person's crisis of faith followed by victory over sin. Popular secular journals feature the same theology usually without explicitly religious language. Persons in crisis take great risks or finally get their lives together, leading to financial success. Horatio Alger stories persist, at times these days portraying young persons who grow up in poor, crime-ridden, drug-infested neighborhoods. Through personal conversion leading to hard work, they are able to escape into the middle class or even great affluence. These are the contemporary parables of the dominant faith of America.

Lisbeth Schorr's world view is the reformed version of this dominant theology. It brings charity to the individual. Today its natural church home is among the mainline denominations. The heroes in its parables are not so much the poor as the committed servants. The doctors who volunteer for free clinics, the teachers who bring love and learning to inner-city schools, or the former president who builds houses for the homeless—these are the heroes of this faith. The unstated truth in these parables of charity is that these people could make a lot more money with fewer hassles if they just ignored those in need. Instead, their faith leads them to serve others.

This theology probably takes its purest form in the fliers denominations produce to encourage giving for missions. Every local United Way campaign produces secular equivalents in their fundraising materials. Various telethons bring the message to the airways. Individuals in need are described, sometimes in embarrassing detail. All they need is a little help from their fellow human beings to be productive members of society. This is the American way of showing concern for our fellow human beings. We reach out with direct services to people we can touch or see. Theologians of this faith find no shortage of scriptural references to support service to others. At their best, they try to address two major weaknesses of an ethic of service by trying to preserve the integrity of those served and to guard against self-righteousness among the servants.

Lawrence Mead's world view sees the current social order as natural and normative. In this it is consistent with conservative versions of natural law theology that see the natural order as created by

God and thus good. When the social order is seen as an extension of nature, work and family are seen as God-given institutions to be preserved. While this static version of natural law predominated in traditional Catholic social teaching, more dynamic interpretations have emerged in recent years.[11] Lutherans continue to respect the orders of the world in their social statements, usually reinforced by an emphasis on the power of human sin. They usually argue that this human tendency to sin requires the discipline offered by authoritative social institutions.[12]

These theologies share many of the assumptions of Mead's world view; the religious right shares his conclusions. In theory many of the leaders of the religious right speak of the freedom of faith, but in practice they fear that the traditional social order is falling apart.[13] At the core of this fear is a commitment to the traditional family. The absence of prayer in school, women's rights, gay rights, abortion, sex education, the teaching of evolution—all seem to challenge the authority structure of the traditional family. For many, welfare does too, by supporting unmarried women and letting fathers escape their responsibility. The theology of the religious right harkens back to a simpler time when husbands were head of the family as described in Scripture.[14]

Frances Fox Piven is clearly the liberation theologian of the welfare debate. She begins with the lived experience of the poor, attempting to see the world from their perspective. Of course, Murray can claim he is trying to look at the world through the eyes of Harold and Phyllis. The difference, of course, is that liberation theology locates the problem in the system, not in the poor. Indeed, Piven's description of the poor as a pool of labor within the capitalist system fits very well with the mainstream of liberation theology.[15] Piven's principle of action, that proposals be judged primarily on the basis of how much the poor get, sounds a lot like "the option for the poor" that liberation theology uses as its central principle of action.

Again, let us not forget that liberation theology, at least its Latin American versions, typically began with study of the Scripture and found plenty of support for their social analysis. For liberation thought, faith is expressed in struggle against the status quo, the principalities and powers, in the name of a greater vision of the good community. Perhaps Piven's championing of the National Welfare Rights Organization best illustrates this analysis. However, throughout her work she advocates conflict and struggle against an unjust system.

THE NATURE OF THEOLOGY

If each of the four world views we have identified has theological parallels, then simply being theological does not seem to settle world view differences. Persons holding any of the four world views can find some theological support for it. Theologies and world views are both plural, not singular, realities. We cannot argue that our theology is the only one any more than we can claim ours is the only possible view of the world. This is just not true. Thus, a necessary part of the task before us is to see how the theology I develop and the view of the world consistent with it relate to these other options. This is messy and at times tedious work, but the truth of our complex world simply requires it. In this particular case, I shall argue that one way to explore these relationships is to identify what is of value in each of the four world views and incorporate that into a comprehensive position that surpasses all four.

The other issue the plurality of theological positions raises is just what counts as theology and religion. Combining what he had learned from Paul Tillich and Alfred North Whitehead, James Luther Adams once defined God as the deepest sense of value in our lives.[16] This primordial experience of value may bring with it reference to specific historical events (the life of Buddha), scriptures (the Constitution of the United States), or institutions (the church). At times people confuse these specific elements of a religious tradition with faith itself. However, what makes something religious is not its connection to particular historical events, scriptures, or institutions. What makes something religious is that it provides a sense of meaning and value to the lives we live. The issue of poverty is in part religious, then, precisely because it raises questions about the meaning and value of our lives. Before we are through we want to explore further just how that is the case.

To be specific about the issue of poverty within the Christian tradition, there can be no doubt about its religious status. Indeed, of all contemporary public issues, historically the Christian Scriptures and Christian churches have been most clear that poverty is a religious issue. In the Hebrew Scriptures, kings were judged on how the poor fared under their rule; prophets focused on the gap between the rich and the poor as a reason for God's judgment. In the Gospels, Jesus associated himself with the poor and offered little comfort to the rich. The early churches raised funds to aid the poor among them. Again and again ever since, official and unofficial ethical statements by churches have centered on the issue of poverty. The overall thrust of this tradition is to place God's presence with the poor and God's judgment upon the affluent who misuse or ignore the needs of the poor.

The principles are clear, but the implications for contemporary practice are much less so. The Scriptures typically condemn the misuse of the poor and encourage various forms of charity. However, they are addressed to a tribal, monarchical, and then imperial political order. They do not envision the concepts of individual rights established during the Enlightenment. They do not speak to modern economic structures or the welfare state. The world views we have identified have been developed and specified in terms of these and many other historical developments. Any attempt to take seriously the ethical issue of poverty in our time must deal with the social realities and the religious insights that have emerged since the first and second centuries. The contemporary public issue of poverty requires a contemporary public theology to deal adequately with its complexity.

There is also a very practical reason why a contemporary public theology is needed. I served for some four years as the governmental affairs staff person for the Illinois Conference of Churches. Whenever we got involved effectively in a political issue, including welfare policy, we found ourselves working with Christians and non-Christians of a wide range of theological orientations. They could not agree on Scripture or doctrine, but they could agree that poverty was wrong and that various particular changes in the welfare system were needed. Yet, they needed to say not only what they wanted done but also why. Moreover, this why came down to the ethical and, finally, religious principles upon which the coalition could agree as a rationale for the policy changes they wanted adopted. For this we had to have a public theology. This theology needed to state a basic understanding of the meaning and purpose of human life that identified realities like poverty as unjust, without seeking agreement on the more specific theological doctrines that divide people. This is what I mean by a contemporary public theology.

One very specific example of such a contemporary public theology is that of Marian Wright Edelman, the president of the Children's Defense Fund. As the aunt, granddaughter, daughter, and sister of Baptist ministers, Edelman can preach. Preach she does but not in a way that appeals only to a single religious tradition. Rather, she speaks of experiences of family and community in terms that are intended to appeal to all Americans. "What unites us is far greater than what divides us as families and friends and Americans and spiritual sojourners on this Earth."[17] She seeks a broad coalition in support of programs that help children, a coalition broad enough to win political battles in a democracy. Yet, Edelman is clear that this is not just a political struggle; it is fundamentally a moral and religious one. *It is a spiritually impoverished nation* that permits infants and children to be the poorest Americans."[18] Her response to this spiritual problem is the image of a nation that, like a loving family, embraces and supports all of its children. "Let us, from whatever faith or ideology or race or community or family type we hail, commit to love and respect and protect every child as God's promise of life in a wayward world."[19] This is a powerful contemporary public theology.

It is tempting to reprint Marian Wright Edelman's "Twenty-Five Lessons for Life" as an adequate theology for addressing poverty and welfare.[20] However, I shall draw upon another strand of thought, process theology, to state a public theology that has much in common with hers. Like Edelman, I shall begin with my own everyday experience to express a theology of human freedom and community. Then, I shall relate this theology to the world views of the four authors we have studied. Next, I shall use this public theology to respond to the five ethical questions we have been asking. With all of this theology and ethical thought pulled together, we shall proceed finally to reconsider poverty, welfare, and current policy options.

CHAPTER NINE

A THEOLOGY OF FREEDOM AND COMMUNITY

Who is any particular person—let us say the one I think I know best—Warren Copeland?[1] First of all, there is both consistency and change in who Warren Copeland is. For instance, my body is the same yet very different from what it once was. At the microscopic level, many a cell has come and gone. Visible to the naked eye, pounds have come and hair has gone. Yet, on a good day this brain and these arms and legs can still coordinate enough and remember enough from hours of practice in my youth to hit a few long jump shots. All in all, my body is itself a society that has seen members come and go and yet has passed down some common characteristics that appear to most people to be me. Each of these moments is me at that one time, preceded by me at earlier times and succeeded by me at later times. Similarly, my mind and personality have changed dramatically over time, and yet there is some thread of consistency in who I am. I am a stream of moments of experience, which are closely connected to one another. Each of those moments is shaped dramatically by its relation to all of the past, especially to its own immediate past. Otherwise my friends would not know me. Yet, change is real. Friends who have not seen me for a long time may not recognize me. Based upon my experience, I think that *all* reality is (like me) constituted by the interrelation among moments of experience and the continual creative addition of new moments of experience related in the same way.[2]

All of this is made more creative and rich for humans because of our capacity to think and act. I have been married to the same woman for over twenty-five years, and she has changed as has my relationship to her. The traditional woman I married got liberated along the way, and that called for changes in me. The young, naive student I fell in love with has become a skilled and committed kindergarten teacher in a school that serves a lot of low-income children. And so I have found myself helping mothers of her students move away from abusive men, sometimes coming to live at our house. I am a very different person as a result. Indeed, most of my recent firsthand experience of poverty has been through the contacts of my wife. We have shared the struggles of our children and the deaths of three of our parents. Neither of us wants to think about life without the other. Clara Coolman Copeland is a big piece of what Warren Copeland has become.

We have lived in the same city for over fifteen years, and yet it and we and our relation to it have changed tremendously over that time. We came to Springfield, Ohio, so that I could teach at Wittenberg University. We chose to live on the south side of town, the wrong side of town according to the usual standards. Most African Americans and Appalachians live on our side of town; the average income is much lower, and the crime rate is much higher. By living where we do, we became a part of a whole set of relationships through our childrens' schools or my coaching baseball or just getting to know our neighbors, quite different from all of the other members of the Wittenberg faculty who live on the north side of town. We have become south-side partisans who are resentful of real and imagined north-side wealth and smugness, and when North High and South High meet, we proudly wear our "Beat North" buttons.

Now I am mayor of all of Springfield and spend a lot of time at receptions and meetings with the movers and shakers of Springfield, most of whom live on the north side. I have also come to know many more northsiders who are not wealthy or not smug. The very nature of my position pushes me to look for realities that unify Springfield rather than divide us. I certainly see as one of my primary goals as mayor the addition and retention of jobs for Springfield. However, since I know how many southsiders feel about the local country club that has no African American members, I simply could not, even (or perhaps especially) as mayor, meet there with the Ohio director of economic development. We need his help to attract and keep jobs here in Springfield, but I know too many of our citizens who find the country club an affront. In the final analysis, my southside roots are just too deep to ignore that. Our past relationships and experiences deeply affect who we are.

I think I am basically the same person I have always been, but my life has certainly changed over time. Sometimes these changes in Warren Copeland have been gradual; sometimes they have been sudden. Sometimes I have thought I exercised significant choice about these changes; sometimes I felt that they were thrust upon me. Am I a product of my relationships? Certainly! Do I exercise some influence upon them? I hope and believe so! How can both be true?

GOD AS PAST REALITY, PRESENT POSSIBILITY, AND FUTURE HOPE

Each moment of my life is formed from the immediate past and that past is critical to what is possible in the present.[3] Most elementally, if a vital part of my body were destroyed in the moments just prior to the present, this could be my last moment as a living person. But the reality beyond my body also helps determine what is possible in the present moment, whether it is the physical environment or other human beings. Similarly, what I become in this present moment will have a lot to say about what is possible in the future. While we often think about this power of the past as a limitation upon our freedom, in fact it also offers to us alternatives we could not create on our own. The final source of this past that we inherit in any moment is the totality of what is—one aspect of God. That past is indeed a gift from God.

Our experience of this power of the past provides strong evidence for behaviorism—that we are products of our environment. What is harder to justify from experience is that there is individual choice. That is what makes the present moment so important. My present moment is shaped not just by the past but also by my experience of possibilities for the future. The final source of what can be is possibility itself, another aspect of God. My sense of possibility helps me shape the present moment in a way that can make a real difference in what is possible in the future.[4] This is also truly a gift from God. This shaping of the present moment is where I make choices; this is the source of my individuality. Now obviously it takes a series of choices over a number of moments to produce the kind of changes in the course of human events that we usually think of as choice. It is critical to remember that at every moment in that chain of choices my alternatives will be significantly affected by the world around me. I make choices, but always choices among possibilities of what I can make of the past that has been presented to me.

As the all-inclusive reality, God includes all that is at any given moment. Thus, God is the source of the past given to us in any particular moment. As that all-inclusive reality, God also encompasses all that is possible at any given moment. Thus, God is the source of the possibilities among which a person chooses in any particular moment. As that all-inclusive reality, God also includes whatever a particular moment produces. Whatever we choose, God will take it into the total reality, which will be God in the next moment, and preserve that choice eternally. Most of us experience these elements of God's presence as loving grace. We inherit a world we have not earned, we are inspired by possibilities beyond us, and our efforts are accepted for what they are. However, we can just as surely experience them as curse or judgment. The world we inherit may limit or threaten us, we may fail to respond to possibilities, or our mistakes may live forever. Our faith in God's love neither means that the world is as good as God wants nor eliminates our responsibility.[5]

STEAM AND DEMOCRACY

Alfred North Whitehead once described change as resulting from a mixture of steam and democracy.[6] Much of the change in our lives results from overpowering compulsions.[7] Some of these compulsions are driven by basic needs such as food, clothing, and love. Someone simply must work to produce goods, if we are to have those goods to consume. A young woman who has access to birth control technology but little money still may want to have a baby because she believes that the baby will be the person to be loved by and to love whom she has never had before. Other compulsions are the result of established patterns of human behavior, what sociologists call the social order. Any U.S. citizen knows that our cities will probably have a part of town where whites live and a part of town where blacks live. This reality we all assume is an aspect of the social order, which deeply shapes our everyday life experience—where we live and where our children go to school—and has proved very hard to change so far. At the same time, our economy is losing well-paying blue-collar jobs, leaving many unemployed or employed at much lower wages. At least in part, these changes are driven by changes in the technologies of production and transportation and communication. This is all steam.

Democracy is our attempt to develop some capacity for human control over these compulsions.[8] At the personal level, this involves being guided by some vision of good action in making choices. The ideal of efficiency leads the business person to find ways to use fewer resources to produce something at lower cost. The desire to be able to provide a loving family leads a young couple to wait before conceiving a child. Some debate over just what ideals are best or what is possible may be involved in each case. However, these are matters primarily of personal choice.

Community choice is much more complicated, because social compulsions are less clear and more spread out and because even more debate about ideals and possibilities is to be expected.[9] Perhaps this is why Whitehead referred to social compulsion (steam) and social choice (democracy). Even if most Americans agree on the ideal of an interracial society, they certainly do not agree that a massive program of scattered-site public housing to facilitate such a society is either necessary or possible. This would require more government involvement in the housing market than most Americans want and more of a threat to affluent, largely white suburbs than they will tolerate. Yet, how else does anyone ever imagine that the growing split between affluent and largely white neighborhoods and poor and predominantly black neighborhoods will ever be overcome? How to bring about full employment is equally controversial. However, failure to find democratic action that is adequate to the challenges of our lives merely leaves compulsion in control over them. We have some capacity for choice, but failure to exercise that capacity or using it poorly does not stop the flow of events.

CHOICE AND SOCIAL ETHICS

This understanding of human experience as limited choice in the midst of change has significant implications for social ethics itself.[10] If we were not in part determined by society there would be no need for us to worry about the nature of that society. Each of us could simply live our lives as freely choosing individuals unaffected by the world around us. The fact that we are shaped by our society makes social ethics necessary. However, if we were unable to make choices on the basis of ideals, social ethics would be impossible. Precisely because we can make decisions that influence the future and because those decisions are shaped by alternative possibilities for what could be, we can act ethically toward our societies. Determinism makes social ethics necessary; freedom makes it possible.

At the same time, any social ethics which does not take seriously compulsions, personal and of the social order, is terribly naive. The force of events overpowers choice more often than not, and generating the personal or social momentum necessary to make significant choices takes real effort. We quite literally must develop the power to confront business as usual on a scale comparable to the powers that be. This requires some considerable political debate and organization. Social ethics, no matter how critical in theory, which fails to come to terms with the reality of social structures and the scale of change necessary to change them, tends to deteriorate into pious personal solutions or self-righteous preaching.

PROCESS THOUGHT AND CHRISTIANITY

The preceding is my attempt to describe what has come to be called process theology in terms of my everyday experience. I believe that process theology provides understandings of freedom and community that can serve as a contemporary public theology for a coalition for positive change in welfare policy. This assumes that people who disagree about their interpretations of Scripture or their understandings of particular doctrines of the churches will find this description of human freedom and community true enough to their experience to base upon it their work with others on an issue like poverty. Only experience can prove this assumption true or false. I also personally believe that this theology is consistent with the Christian tradition. Others have written much more extensively on this matter, but let me note a few basic elements of this connection.[11]

The Christian tradition speaks of humans as created in the image of God. If the basic character of God is to create, we must see our basic human capacity as acting creatively. This is how humans are described in process thought. The Christian tradition consistently speaks of humans as members of communities. It is difficult to find in that tradition support for isolated individuals who are not responsible to and for others. This is entirely consistent with the description of individuality within community that process thought gives. Finally, Christians are called to challenge the principalities and powers for the sake of love and justice. This is what Whitehead means by the struggle between steam and democracy. This commonality between process theology and the Christian tradition should come as no surprise since the originators of the former were steeped in the latter. They assumed they were searching for contemporary ways to understand ancient truths.

THE ETHICAL QUESTIONS REFORMULATED

What does this theology of the human condition as a mix of social inheritance and individual choice have to say about the five fundamental ethical questions that arose as we read different interpretations of poverty? Quite a bit, I think.

1. Individuality—To what extent and how can individuals be self-determining?

Even in the above description of human experience we have moved a long way down the path of answering this question. Clearly there is no such thing as an isolated individual. What we are is formed out of the world we share with other human beings. These relationships dramatically shape the choices we have at any given time. Many courses of action are not real possibilities for us, given the communities from which we come. My father owned and operated a small upholstery shop in a blue-collar railroad town. The railroad men would sit around my dad's shop on the old furniture waiting to be fixed. As a boy whose job it was to clean out the shop and to do some upholstery so simple I could not mess it up, I learned a certain philosophy of life from those railroad guys. Key to that philosophy was a sarcastic distrust of those with power and money and a respect for everyday common sense. My two older brothers came up through the same experience of the upholstery shop, and so we shared that view of the world. For good or ill, that perspective on life still influences the way I think and act nearly forty years later. Positively, this means that I respect the wisdom of the working class more than many people expect who assume that college professors are elitists with their heads in the clouds. Negatively, we three brothers shared a rough-and-tumble, sarcastic sense of humor that the women we married sometimes experienced as just plain mean. We humans are indelibly shaped by our relationship to the world around us.

However, we do make choices from the possibilities given to us. For all we three Copeland brothers had in common, we went in very different directions in our lives—an upholsterer, an insurance agent, and a college professor. We developed a wide variety of moral commitments and political views. Part of those differences came from different influences upon us. Bob went off to the army, Dave to radio school, and I to college and seminary and graduate school. However, part also came from choices we made about what to do with the possibilities placed before us. Bob married Lee and joined my father's upholstering shop under the G.I. bill. Dave went south as a disc jockey and met and married Ruth. I became active in the campus civil rights organization and married Clara. This is what self-determination means, putting our unique stamp upon what we are given and thus making a creative contribution to future possibilities. The ideals that inspire this self-determination are God's gift to individuality. We humans are certainly not isolated individuals nor self-made in any simple sense, yet we can play a unique role not only in determining ourselves but also the course of history itself. No one else will ever find themselves in exactly the same place and time as we do in each moment of our lives.[12]

2. Community—To what extent and how can communities contribute to human well-being?

From what we have already said it is clear that communities have a lot to say about who we are. Yet this view of human life understands community in a particular way. Precisely because I do have some capacity to make choices based on the value I perceive, I contribute to what the community becomes in the future. Community then can be a vibrant, changing set of relations among individuals who are all capable of making some unique contribution to the future. The community I receive from the past is the sum total of past decisions to which I add my contribution. If we are lucky, we belong to a community—good friends, a church school class, or a political action group—composed of people with strong convictions but also the willingness to listen to one another. Such a community shapes us while accepting our unique contribution to the whole. The ultimate model of such a community is a God who is the source of creativity and the loving recipient of what is created.[13]

This dynamic, pluralistic understanding of community is at some distance from views of community we have read, which stress conformity and order—and for good reason. Communities are also problems. Friends can betray us, churches can split into divisive factions, and political action can deteriorate into personality cults. Most of all, whether out of fear or mere loss of vision, communities can require us to think and to act like everyone else or risk exclusion. At their worst, communities may use force or terror to enforce this conformity.

This view of ideal relation between individuality and community leads us to certain conclusions about what counts as good individuality and good community. The most humanly enriching community is one that provides the most intense and diverse experience to individuals and receives and appreciates the novelty each individual has to offer back to the community. The ideal is for a community to support and tolerate just as strong a mix of unique contributions as possible without lapsing into chaos. The highest purpose for the individual is to contribute as much value and intensity to the community as possible. A richly diverse community makes genuine individuality possible; unique individuals contribute to such a community. When this is true, we do not have to choose between individuality and community because they complement each other. To try to force a choice between them is bad theology.

3. Worth—To what extent and how are human beings worthy of respect and support by their mere existence?

What we are at any moment we receive from the world. We are not responsible for having created most of that world, whether good or bad. A child is born to two loving parents. Together and separately they have their problems and their strengths, but they have created a home into which that child is born and which shapes very much what that child is to become. Happily these parents love that child even when it cries at 2:00 A.M. from colic. That child has not earned such love any more than another child deserves to be slapped or shaken for crying in the middle of the night. If we are lucky, our world supports our development. This is the initial meaning of grace.

James Luther Adams had suggested that the best of the Christian faith is expressed in the father welcoming the prodigal son home. With his arms wrapped around this son who has wasted his inheritance and thus forfeited his claim to deserve the father's love, the father expresses another dimension of grace—acceptance.[14] When the individual acts, that action is accepted back into the world. Strong or weak, that contribution becomes part of the stuff from which the future will be made. So there is grace in both what we receive from the world and in the world taking what we give back. We earn neither; both are the gift of God.

And yet in the moment we choose, we take responsibility. What value we are able to make of what we are given and therefore what we are able to contribute back is to our credit or blame. The young man who takes responsibility for the baby he has helped make, even though he does not have much money, deserves more credit than another young man equally poor who is not a father to his child. Neither may deserve the poverty in which they find themselves and both remain human beings to be respected regardless of what they do. However, the contribution of the father who chooses to help his child has added something of value, no matter how small, to the world. Indeed, he has provided some grace for that young life he helped create. In sum, we cannot do enough to earn the right to be supported and respected, but what we do does make a difference. We are not saved by works, but in gratitude for what we have received we can add to the grace in the world.

4. Motivation—To what extent and how can humans act on the basis of more than short-term self-interest?

Whether we celebrate it as motivation or decry it as greed, self-interest is dominant in our explanations of why people do what they do, and anyone who does not recognize it at work in human behavior is dangerously naive. This is what theologians call sin. In fact, we may emphasize the power of self-interest so much that we forget about all that we do for others every day, let alone what others do for us. Cynicism is widespread. In the materials we have read, this question of human nature generally comes up in two forms: the importance of economic incentives and the likelihood of taxpayer resistance to welfare expenditures.

According to our theology of freedom and community, the question comes down to whether humans will respond to the positive lure of greater possibilities for the future or reject that lure in the name of some lesser value. Putting the motivation issue more directly, will people respond to positive incentives to achieve greater purposes, or must they be punished in order for them to change behavior? Theologically, the question is whether sin is essentially an affirmation of me against others and finally God or whether it is essentially a denial, a shrinking back, from what we could become.[15] Expressed in psychological terms, is the problem too much self-interest or too weak a self-concept? The answer may be different depending on how much power we have been free to exercise in our lives; self-interest is usually the problem for those who have had power, and self-concept for those who have not. However, the understanding of human action I have described would suggest that what we need most is greater purposes and the capacity to achieve them. Most of the time, we settle for less than we can be rather than think too highly of ourselves. This is especially true for those like the poor who must worry about their very survival.

Will people pay more taxes to help those less fortunate than themselves? Probably not, as long as they believe that they can neatly separate their destiny from that of those to be helped. However, the description of human action we have developed makes clear that we share the world with our fellow human beings. The quality of my future is dependent in significant part upon the contributions of others. If others are unable to contribute as much to the world as they might—unable to support and care for their children, unable to work at a productive job, or unable to join with their neighbors to make their neighborhood livable—then I am worse off. Are people able to understand these shared interests enough to pay more taxes or to forgo some benefits? Sometimes we are, and sometimes we are not. That is decided by human choice, and that choice depends in part on whether we believe there are practical and effective means of addressing our common needs.

5. Hope—To what extent and how are current negative patterns of interaction and power subject to change?

Change is certain when we understand reality to be a chain of moments each following upon the past. So, the real question is not whether there is change but rather whether genuine novelty is introduced by the decision made in a given moment about what elements to continue from the past and in what relation to each other. If we are trying to predict the future and our goal is to be correct as often as possible, the safest prediction is that the future will be pretty much like the past. Mostly, it probably will be. However, what is most interesting is precisely those events that dramatically shift the flow of events; such events are what we usually mean by history. We dare not ignore the power of inheritance, neither should we dismiss the emergence of novelty.

However, this novelty can make matters worse just as easily as better. If there is real choice in human affairs then there can be no guarantee of improvement. This chance of deterioration is what makes social stability look pretty good at times. What is assured is that what is true or beautiful or just is such whether or not it is also successful. That is precisely why we find truth, beauty, and justice so attractive as ideals for human action, and therein lies our final hope, one more gift from God. But the understanding of human action we have developed also assures us that action for the sake of truth, beauty, or justice has value in at least giving them some concrete form that can be passed on to the future. In so doing we make those ideals more real for those for whom our present becomes the past from which they choose. How many of us have been inspired by past attempts to establish justice, even those that failed? At this time in the history of the United States when so many of us seem to believe that what we do for truth, beauty, or justice makes no difference, this assurance that our action has meaning may be the hope we need the most.

In one of the classic sections in Alfred North Whitehead's *Adventures of Ideas,* he traces how freedom became a powerful enough ideal to end slavery.[16] From the Greeks and Jesus to Methodists and Quakers, he shows how so many contributed to the increasing social power of this idea of freedom. What is terribly important is that many of the contributions along the way were relatively unknown or the subject of ridicule in their own time and yet shaped and swayed the future. They gave new form and meaning to this ideal of freedom that could be picked up, expanded upon, and finally realized by succeeding generations. Similar tales can be told of all those unknown people considered failures, even in their own minds, who laid the groundwork for all great movements of social change. People who act for the sake of truth, beauty, or justice have every reason to hope that they may indeed overcome someday.

THE FOUR POSITIONS REVISITED

What now can we say about the four positions we have identified and analyzed, based upon the basic understanding of human action and its implication for the ethical questions our reading of these positions have raised? Once again, hopefully quite a bit.

Clearly our reading of the human condition does not square with the fully independent individual Murray seeks. We are shaped by our communities much more than Murray allows, and at our best we contribute back to those communities. Murray's insistence that we must earn our way in this world flies in the face of the obvious reality that, for good or ill, our world makes us who we are to a great extent. The only thing that Murray expects to move poor people is the gritty reality of their need to survive on their own effort; no positive motivation here. Finally, Murray expects poor people, like his famous Harold and Phyllis, to remain poor. Nothing much will change for them except the satisfaction of knowing that they have earned their poverty. He seems to think that is hope. Yet, in the final analysis we had better not dismiss too quickly Murray's willingness to let people decide for themselves. At its best, that commitment is the beginning of the respect personal uniqueness deserves and requires.

Schorr certainly recognizes the power of social relations in shaping individuals, and she states that the social services she advocates must be accompanied by basic changes in the social structure. However, she is strangely inarticulate about what structural changes she has in mind or how they will come about. Sooner or later the recipients of her social services will need jobs and livable neighborhoods. It also remains finally unclear just what effort Schorr expects from the recipients of the social services. How will these services help recipients accept responsibility? She seems similarly naive both about how fully people will develop into contributing adults with a little help and about how easily taxpayers will agree to pay for these programs. Finally, she seems overconfident that we know how to solve our problems. Perhaps all of this overconfidence flows from her underes-timation of the power of social structures. Yet, Schorr's strength lies in her recognition that social situations close down or open up our personal futures and that restriction of human possibility is an issue for all of us. Good societies require effective individuals.

In a real sense Mead is less democratic than Murray. Murray believes that once we get government out of the way nearly all individuals are able to do for themselves. Mead, on the other hand, feels a significant group of the poor will act like the rest of us only if the government forces them to do so. There is no grace in Mead. In fact, he doubles the judgment on the poor. As individuals, they are to blame for their situation, and yet society must force them to change. For him, the poor cannot be motivated to work by positive incentives; they must be punished if they will not behave. Typical of the true conservative, Mead does not hold out much hope for change. He seeks control over feared chaos much more than progress. Yet, Mead's recognition that communities must hang together for them to support and appreciate people's contributions is true. Social chaos is more likely to lead to authoritarian responses than to creativity. Communities dare not deteriorate into chaos even as they seek to be as pluralistic as possible.

Piven is consistent in a number of ways with the theology of the human condition I have developed. She takes the social context very seriously, and yet she seeks a community that not only allows a lot of dissent but also involves constant conflict. Clearly she does not blame the poor for their poverty, so much so that she may not fully recognize the corrosive effects that poverty has on the human dignity she prizes. Piven is brutally realistic about how the self-interest of the powerful undergirds the present social structure and about how interests, not simply good intentions, must fuel any movement for change. In all these ways, she has much in common with our theology of freedom and community, more than any of the other three positions. However, she describes the power of the elite as so dominant as to make significant change nearly impossible. As a result she generally encourages the poor to take what they can get rather than what they need. She seems to be a bit less realistic about the continuing need for incentives for efforts. If the welfare system merely alternates between relatively generous responses to disorder and cutbacks in assistance when order is restored as Piven describes, then the system itself must be changed. Yet Piven does not expect any fundamental changes. That leaves only hope for limited change in return for a lot of conflict and pain.

In sum, based on our theology of freedom and community we can see something of value in the basic assumptions of each of these four world views. At their best each recognizes part of the fundamental human reality we have described. However, none brings these realities together in the dynamic and comprehensive way our theology does. Thus, they each express only a part of the whole story of human freedom and community, which I have tried to articulate. This more comprehensive theology has also allowed us to respond more adequately to the five ethical questions we have posed. Now, it is time to ask how this theology and ethics help us understand poverty in its full human meaning. Then, we shall consider what it has to say generally about welfare policy. That will bring us finally to current policy possibilities.

CHAPTER TEN

UNDERSTANDING THE HUMAN MEANING OF POVERTY: WILLIAM JULIUS WILSON AND BEYOND

G ive me your tired, your poor, your huddled masses yearning to breathe free."[1] America understands itself to be the land of the formerly poor. Former peasants become the homesteaders, perhaps still poor but now poor landowners. Poor immigrants from Europe settle in an American urban slum and go to work in sweatshops. They form a union and join an urban political machine, and they (or probably their children) end up in a middle-class suburb. Poor black farmhands are pushed off Southern plantations because they are not needed with the arrival of tractors, cultivators, and harvesters and head north to cities with factories. At first they are used as strikebreakers but in time they break into the unions and send their kids off to college. This is the American dream—poor people moving up to the middle class or beyond. This is what America believes is its meaning in the world.

POVERTY GETS STUBBORN

So it is not insignificant that people across the ideological spectrum seem to believe poverty is becoming a more stubborn American reality. In his last book on the subject that made him famous, Michael Harrington described a change in the nature of poverty, which he described in something like the following terms.[2] When poor immigrants arrived in American cities around 1900, they found themselves living in a crowded tenement with lousy living conditions. However, they also found growing factories hiring people with strong backs without much regard to the amount of their education or even whether they spoke English. In time these workers formed and fought for unions and saw their wages rise to a level high enough that they could join the middle class. For generations this remained the primary road out of poverty in the United States. According to Harrington, that road is now closed. Well-paying blue-collar jobs are disappearing, taking with them a portion of the middle class and certainly eliminating opportunity for poor people. These well-paying blue-collar jobs are being replaced by low-paying, non-union manufacturing and service jobs or by higher-paying jobs that require education beyond high school. The new poor lack the education to get the well-paying jobs and, therefore, face a future of low-paying jobs with little or no potential for a better job later.

At the other end of the ideological spectrum are a range of conservatives like Murray and Mead who also believe there is a new poverty.[3] The new poverty they see, however, is typified by generations on welfare. What they fear is that children grow up on welfare learning that it, rather than work, is the most dependable source of income. Once upon a time, they say, welfare was just a temporary helping hand to those between jobs who left it behind as soon as they found a new job. Now, far too many poor girls learn to expect that they will grow up to have children without marrying and then live off the welfare system, and far too many poor boys assume they will grow up to live off women on welfare rather than to marry, go to work, and support their families. According to Murray and Mead, this new poverty from which people do not expect to escape is just the opposite of the American dream.

Harrington and Murray and Mead and all those who hold ideological positions somewhere between them have facts to back the view that the nature of poverty in America has changed. It is likely that they are all on to something, even if they interpret it very differently. What we want to examine more fully here are the dynamics that have led to these new realities and then to explore the full human meaning of poverty that emerges from our theology of freedom and community. To begin that process, we must become familiar with the most influential interpretation of contemporary poverty in the United States, that of William Julius Wilson. This University of Chicago sociologist's *The Truly Disadvantaged* is the book anyone thinking about poverty today must take into account.[4] We can agree or disagree with Wilson, but we dare not ignore him.

WILLIAM JULIUS WILSON'S ANALYSIS

Wilson believes there are complex reasons for what he calls the "tangle of pathology" in the inner cities of America, which he illustrates most dramatically with statistics on violent crime and on family dissolution and welfare.[5] In part it is the result of a history of discrimination, especially against African Americans. Second, blacks migrated to cities too late to get in on the ground floor of the upward mobility provided by well-paying manufacturing jobs. Third, inner cities today are young, and young people (especially teens) always have created more social problems such as crime. In some cases the young have reached a critical mass in poor communities, leaving everyone else afraid of them. Fourth, Wilson shares the view of basic economic trends described earlier by Harrington. Jobs, and especially well-paying jobs for those with less education, are disappearing and the young people in inner cities lack the education necessary to get better jobs. All four of these realities have played a significant role in creating the new face of poverty in America.[6]

However, Wilson stresses a fifth factor which has come to be identified as the core of his analysis.[7] As Wilson tells it, the social and economic geography of contemporary American cities has changed significantly. Poor neighborhoods, and especially African American ones, have usually included many working-class and middle-class residents in the past. With the growth of suburbs and, paradoxically, with the success of the Civil Rights Movement for African Americans, working-class and middle-class residents moved out of inner-city neighborhoods. When they did they took with them three very important social realities—contacts, role models, and institutions.

Middle-class job searchers are told to network, to figure out who they know who might help them get a job. Similarly, poor kids need someone in the apartment building who knows jobs are opening up at work or someone down the block who is starting a yard-care business, but the people with those contacts have moved out of the neighborhood. Middle-class kids see their parents go to work and get ahead. Similarly, poor kids need role models, but their parents are on welfare or in a dead-end job, and the more successful neighbors have moved out of the neighborhood. Middle-class neighborhoods are marked by good schools, parks, recreation centers and thriving churches, shopping centers, and supermarkets. When the working class and middle class moved out, these institutions went with them, usually leaving behind vacant buildings or weakened institutions. For instance, schools that serve the middle class are likely to have stronger parent groups, better facilities, and better or less burned-out teachers. Remember, education increasingly decides the economic future of children, particularly poor children.

Wilson calls this change in the social and economic geography of cities social isolation. He uses census data for Chicago to show that the concentration of poverty has been growing over the past twenty or so years. Not only is the percentage of poor people in inner-city census tracts increasing but such tracts are increasingly surrounded by similar poverty tracts. The poor are becoming increasingly concentrated at a growing distance from the nonpoor. This is the new shape of poverty, which is quite consistent with the observations of those from various ideological positions that the nature of poverty has changed.

WELFARE AND FAMILIES

When Wilson applies his analysis to family dissolution and welfare dependency, he begins with some facts often ignored. First of all, the number of young women (including African Americans) having babies has not increased. We seem to forget just how many very young women had babies in past generations when there was little expectation that people should stay in school as long as today. What has happened is that older women, including married ones, are having far fewer babies. Therefore the *percentage* of babies born to young, unmarried women has increased dramatically. The problem is just as real, but it is not caused by young people having more babies than in the past.[8]

Murray and Mead suggest that the percentage of poor families without an adult male has increased because welfare is so generous or is given so irresponsibly. Wilson argues instead that poor women do not marry because they cannot find a man to support the family.

With so many poor young males, particularly African American ones, either in jail or unemployed, there are not many men from which to choose. He calls the number of men able to support a family the "male marriageable pool" and says it is drying up in poor neighborhoods.[9] Given the welfare system in the United States in which each state sets its own benefit levels, it is possible to test whether the number of female-headed households correlates with the level of welfare benefits. Is the percentage of female-headed households higher in high-benefit states and lower in low-benefit states? Alternatively, is the percentage of female-headed households higher in states of high youth unemployment and lower in states of low youth unemployment? In spite of what Murray and Mead and probably the majority of Americans may believe, Wilson thinks the facts are clear—female-headed households do not correlate with welfare but do generally correlate with youth unemployment.[10]

The conclusion Wilson draws from his analysis and the data he has studied is that the basic need is jobs primarily for young men, not tougher welfare regulations aimed primarily at young women. Where Wilson has been most controversial is in suggesting that these problems have to do with class, not race, and that solutions should not be based on race. In a previous book,[11] he argued that the educated black middle class was doing pretty well with the help of the civil rights progress of the sixties. He clearly recognizes that because of historical racial discrimination African Americans are more likely to be poor. However, in the present situation, Wilson believes poverty, not racial discrimination, is the key problem to be addressed.

In terms of principles for action, Wilson believes this reality pushes us to what he calls the principle of equality of life chances.[12] The Civil Rights Movement of the sixties was based primarily on the principle of the rights of minority individuals to sit where they wanted on the bus, to go to the same school as whites, to eat where they wanted, or to vote. It was a success in opening doors to those with the credentials to use the individual opportunities opened up but left behind the poor who did not have those credentials. An alternative principle, preferential treatment of minority groups, was proposed as a corrective. Affirmative action and setting aside a portion of highway funds for minority construction companies are examples of policies based on this principle. While these policies generate a lot of opposition, they also help primarily the most advantaged members of the minority group. If the goal is to help those most in need then that is exactly what must be the principle, what Wilson calls the principle of equality of life chances. Put simply, regardless of the accident of birth, every person should have basically the same chance of success in life. For Wilson, the most important policy under such a principle is full employment and particularly jobs for the poor.

A criticism of Wilson's stress on the isolation of the underclass centers primarily on whether he has overgeneralized.[13] There are neighborhoods that fit Wilson's description and in those neighborhoods social isolation of the sort he details may be a major factor in the problems of that neighborhood. However, critics say only a small percentage of poor Americans (5 percent by one study) and a very small portion of Americans (1 percent by the same study) live in such neighborhoods. So, the critics say, Wilson has identified a significant social problem, but it is not the problem typical of poverty in America. So what? Well, it may be that the vast majority of the poor can be included in the mainstream of American society without trying to address the peculiar and very difficult problems of the underclass neighborhood. Or, on the contrary, policies aimed at the specific problems of underclass neighborhoods may miss most of the poor. Interestingly, critics from this angle tend to share Wilson's advocacy of full employment as the most significant single policy for dealing with poverty. However, they recognize that full employment may well help those who do not live in underclass neighborhoods more than those who do.

THREE ALTERNATIVE VIEWS OF POVERTY

Before we use our theology of freedom and community to explore the full human meaning of poverty, we should remind ourselves that Wilson's is not the only way of understanding poverty. Wilson himself describes three different views of poverty. Given what we have read from our four experts on poverty we can fill out Wilson's three categories much more fully than he does himself.

Culture of Poverty

The first of these three interpretations of poverty is usually called the *culture of poverty* view.[14] According to it the poor learn values that are different from those of the majority, and these values make it hard for them to escape poverty. Most people believe that we should work to support our families. The poor value getting out of work more than working and are willing to let the government support their children. Those who hold this view do not necessarily have to blame the poor for holding these values. A girl is born to a mother on welfare. She never knows her father or only knows him as a man who visits from time to time. Her mother is supported by government, not by her father. When she gets older, why should she expect to marry the father of her child or expect him to support them?

Of the four people we have discussed, Charles Murray and Lawrence Mead hold this view in somewhat different forms. Someone like Murray believes that economic incentives reinforce good or bad values. If market incentives are allowed to operate, the values of work and family will take over.[15] Mead believes it will take much more than a change in incentives to overcome the distance between mainstream values and the values of the poor. He believes that poor children raised in a culture of poverty internalize its values so completely that it shapes how they act regardless of the usual incentives. So, when jobs are available, poor people do not take them because they do not value work and do not feel responsible for supporting their children.[16]

When politicians emphasize the work ethic and family values as the key to dealing with poverty, they are using the culture of poverty analysis. It has become the dominant rationale for conservative welfare policy in the nineties. Some opponents of welfare like Murray use it to argue that poverty can only be solved by the poor themselves changing their values, and government should stay out of it. Others like Mead use the same basic analysis to argue for more government action in order to change the culture of poverty. For them, negative values are so deeply imbedded in the poor and government responsibility for basic values so clear, that government must act. In both cases the focus is on changing the poor, not on changing society.

Culture is more difficult to change than behavior. As a result, deeply ingrained values may cause programs aimed at changing behavior, such as job training and employment programs, to fail. There is a version of this view that is much less conservative than either Murray or Mead. It argues that poor people are no more to blame for the culture they inherit than for their social situation.[17] Nevertheless,

151

all advocates of the culture of poverty view contend that policy must address cultural beliefs and not just economic opportunity.

Opportunity Theory

The opposite of the culture of poverty view is opportunity theory.[18] By this theory, poor people share exactly the same values and goals as everyone else in society. The problem is that their odds of achieving those goals by the means considered legitimate by the broader society are not very good. A poor teen sees people on his television enjoying the pleasure of middle-class life, say a sports car. Living in a poor neighborhood with an inadequate school and little job opportunity, that teen's best chance of owning a sports car may well be by selling drugs. Even if that is not true, he probably knows at least one drug dealer with a new sports car. That young man has exactly the same values and goals as most people his age, but he may well choose an alternative means that fits better with his social situation, such as selling drugs, for achieving them.[19]

Schorr and Piven hold this view in somewhat different ways. Schorr believes that, with opportunity in the form of various kinds of support, poor people can develop into successes. Harold needs job training; Phyllis needs prenatal care; their child needs health care, child care, and a good education; they may all need family counseling. Throughout, her goal is to help people develop a positive sense of self through positive support.[20] The solution to poverty according to Piven is not to change the values of the poor but rather to change the economic and social system so that poor people have the same opportunity to succeed as the rest of us. Poor people are poor because they do not have enough money, not because they lack the proper motivation or values. This capitalist society has failed Harold and Phyllis because it needs a pool of cheap labor in order to keep wages down and profits up. The blame clearly lies with society, not with the poor, and there is no need to change poor people.[21]

Value-Stretch

The third view of poverty, that held by Wilson, is sometimes called the value-stretch position. Wilson would agree that all of us, including the poor, do develop values that make sense of our social situation and that these values do take on some life of their own. The classic study of this position is *Tally's Corner* by Elliot Liebow.[22] Liebow hung out on a street corner of a poor neighborhood in Washington, D.C., and got to know the men who frequented the carryout on the corner. Liebow illustrates in detail his thesis that those men begin with the same views as most Americans, but adjust their values to the reality of their lives. For instance they dream of getting that good job that will be the ticket to the middle class. What they get instead are the low-paying, dead-end jobs available to men like them. Over time they adjust their values to this reality, coming to accept and justify that reality by coming to see jobs as merely short-term arrangements to get money for a particular purpose. This is what Liebow calls value-stretch from a previous article on the topic by Hyman Rodman.[23] This alternate value does in fact get in the way of these men taking advantage of what new job opportunities might come along.

This third view recognizes that poor people may hold values different from the mainstream. Wilson even agrees that "some cultural traits may in fact take on a life for a period of time of their own and thereby become a constraining or liberating factor in the life of certain individuals and groups in the inner city."[24] However, he believes these values arose from the social and economic situation and will change when that situation changes, although it may take time for them to fade. The implications for poverty policy are clear to Wilson. Policy should seek to change the social and economic conditions that led to the formation of the alternative values rather than aim policy directly at the values, as proposed by Mead. For Wilson this means ending the social isolation through full employment rather than joining Mead in requiring the low-wage dead-end jobs, which led to the formation of the alternative values in the first place.

THEOLOGY AND POVERTY

On the basis of our theology of freedom and community, it is impossible to think of anyone as self-made in any simple sense. Each moment of our life is formed out of the past we inherit. An eight-year-old boy growing up in the combat zone of a divorce between an abusive father and a mother who was abused herself as a child inherits a very different past than the daughter of two loving, happily married parents. If that eight-year-old also attends a school where a lot of other kids are disruptive, teachers are burning out, and no one expects all that much from kids like him, he will find it hard to learn as much as the young girl attending a warm, orderly school where kids are expected to learn. Now, a few children in the difficult situation described will survive and even prosper perhaps because of a loving parent or grandparent or a talented teacher or reasons unknown. Likewise, a few children in the supportive situation described will have a tough time in life either because they are spoiled or because there are hidden problems. However we all know that the odds of success are very different because of what children inherit from the world around them. That is why nearly all parents want their children to grow up in positive environments.

Some say it is all a matter of motivation, an easy position for those who can get ahead with relatively little effort. But from where does motivation itself come? Does it not tend to develop in us precisely because we learn that when we make an effort, our world rewards us? If our hard work does not seem to bring positive results, then our motivation may wane or lead us in directions society does not like, such as crime. In any event, motivation is itself inherited, in part, from the world around us. While this may seem fairly obvious when we talk about the immediate effect of parents on children, it is also true of broader influences like those Wilson describes. Neighborhoods where the parks are controlled by drug dealers, the community center is closed, the schools do not work, and there is no work for parents are as hard on kids as their parents are. Such neighborhoods are a part of an entire urban social landscape shaped by interstate highways, intercity drug trade, and changes in the national and world economy. In sum, the world we inherit is as specific as our father's mental state and as systemic as the world economy, and it shapes us.

Finally, and perhaps most important for our understanding of poverty, the influence of the world upon us does not stop when we are no longer kids. We do not blame poor kids for their poverty, but we do generally blame poor adults, *and* they usually blame themselves. This creates policy schizophrenia because most Americans want to help poor children and, at the same time, to punish the poor adults with whom they live. To begin with, most poor adults were poor children, and in a world where our employment fate is increasingly decided by our success as a child in school, having been a poor child makes it much more likely we will become a poor adult. Moreover, our world is not all that kind to poor adults who typically lack job skills or are responsible for supporting and caring for children on their own. Even Murray describes the choices that face Harold and Phyllis in terms that do not leave them any very good options.[25] If we are to be consistent with our theology of freedom and community, we must recognize the extent to which poor people must deal with a social world that certainly does not support them and may even encourage their destruction.

INDIVIDUALITY

Yet, there remains a voice within us that values self-determination and self-sufficiency in our personal lives and says to us that it would be better if adults could do for themselves. We should not ignore that voice as long as we recognize the limits of self-determination and thus of responsibility (or blame). Our theology of freedom and community affirms the value of individuals taking the world that is given to them in any particular moment and making the best they can of it.[26] This is why poverty is a deeply personal problem. To be poor is to suffer often from a lack of food, shelter, medical care, or other essentials. To be poor is to have not enough money to provide for your children's basic needs, let alone those things that most other kids have. However, the greatest personal loss that poverty causes is the inability to make one's own way in life. The loss of control and self-worth that comes with poverty, and especially with having to ask for help, is deeper than any material wants. This personal meaning of poverty makes it much less possible for poor people to make the best of what they inherit from the world.

The plight of the poor is not just to suffer but to suffer without notice except in terms of their capacity to survive. Survival may be a major achievement for many poor people who spend hours in line at various assistance programs or working at low-paying jobs in order to survive. The peculiarly human curse of poverty is that humans are reduced to the lowest common denominator of mere existence. One need only reflect a moment upon conversations about poor people among those who are not poor to notice that little attention is paid to the hopes and dreams and goals and effort of poor people. They become abstract beings to be pitied or resented, but not to be known as humans. The poor seldom appear in these conversations as truly human, seldom realize uniquely human capacities. As Hannah Arendt put it:

> Poverty is more than deprivation, it is a state of constant want and acute misery whose ignominy consists in its dehumanizing force; poverty is abject because it puts men [sic] under the absolute dictate of their bodies, that is, under the absolute dictate of necessity.[27]

The capacity to rise above necessity to make a creative contribution to the future requires a sense of our selves as shapers of reality. Our theology of freedom and community clearly implies that any attempt to deal with poverty should seek to allow poor people to develop a greater capacity for relative self-determination as they get more money.

COMMUNITY

Mead and Wilson among others are quite right to emphasize that to be poor is to be separated from the community. The most basic exclusion is from the economic system itself, but money buys participation in much of what it means to be American. In part, this has always been true because our public services are not as developed as most nations of our wealth, but many public services have deteriorated in recent years, especially at the state and local level. Financially strapped school systems require students to pay for more and more of their books and supplies and field trips and extracurricular activities. Libraries have been closed, recreation programs cut back or replaced by programs with fees, homeowners are assessed for more and more city services. As Wilson has made clear, the neighborhoods whose institutions decline the most are precisely those where the poor live. The poor, young and old, are left with ugly choices between necessities and participation in the social activities common to the mainstream.

In a society that claims to be democratic, the political significance of this social exclusion cannot be dismissed. Clearly the poor do not vote in large numbers, but this is but the simplest measure of a much deeper problem. Citizens govern in part through a whole series of associations and organizations, everything from the Mobile Home

Dealers Association to the Audubon Society or the National Association of Manufacturers to the National Organization of Women. By and large the poor do not belong to such groups. Even the National Welfare Rights Organization, never a major political power but at least a voice, has fallen on hard times in recent years. How, then, do poor people act to make their neighborhood safe or their school better or their job safe in a world where they are up against very powerful forces—very heavy steam? They do not! These are fundamental questions if we truly prize democracy.

It is easy enough to conceive of a permanent underclass, one which is provided an income or required to work but not a part of the institutions of the social life that the rest of us take for granted. Some of the authors we have read believe we have already reached that point. Certainly the human geography of our cities gives us little reason for hope. We are a society separated by race and income and with little expressed will to change. Any serious attempt to deal with poverty will need to allow and even assist the poor to take an active part in the organizational life of our society. Even more threatening to most of us, we are going to have to reconsider the nature of our communities and change them so that there is in fact a place for everyone. If we are to do so, we will undoubtedly have to recognize how our entire communities are impoverished when some are excluded and just how much richer and more exciting they would be if everyone were fully able to contribute to them.

This is precisely what our theology of freedom and community suggests. The world provides significant limits on what we can do in any moment. However, the world also changes because we act; it is enriched by whatever we do of value. The more persons there are who make creative contributions to this world, the richer it becomes for all. Just think of the creative talent channeled each day in poor communities into illegal activities. The imagination and effort that poor people put into working the system for as much help as possible alone could make the world so much more interesting and exciting if it were expressed in more legitimate ways. We all have something to gain of genuine human value from all people being able to contribute to the world we share. Poverty helps keep that from happening.

WORTH

Many poor people do things that destroy themselves and others. Those of us who are not poor do many of the same things but often get away with them because we can afford to clean up the mess we cause. Yet rates of homicide and other crimes against people, of domestic violence, and of serious addictions make clear that Wilson is correct that there is serious pathology in poor neighborhoods. Moreover, many of us fear that as long as the pain and death is contained within poor neighborhoods, the greater society is not vitally concerned. Are poor persons just not worth as much concern from the rest of us? Much greater numbers of the poor never show up in such statistics, but simply lack the sense of self necessary to improve their situation. To be poor is to be of little recognized value to yourself or to others. In a society where our accepted measure of human value is what we want and where wealth allows us to buy what we want, wealth becomes the accepted measure of worth. Obviously, the poor do not measure up very well. Perhaps this question of worth is the one most easily recognized as religious.

If we shift our view of worth from wealth possessed to the capacity to contribute positively to the flow of events, money remains significant. Our capacity to contribute is handicapped if we must constantly be concerned with day-to-day survival. If the social institutions (like schools and neighborhoods and jobs) necessary for us to develop our human capacities are not available or are second-class, we will not be able to contribute as much. However, we do not need to have exactly the same wealth as the next person. Indeed, wealthy people too busy making money to have a family life or participate in the community are no better off in human worth, even if they are more physically comfortable, than a person who is poor. Efforts to deal with poverty must address this issue of worth, and our odds of addressing the issue are probably dependent upon all of us recognizing some greater measure of human value than money.

MOTIVATION

Are people poor because they lack the healthy self-interest that we usually call motivation? Even Murray does not think so. Rather,

Harold and Phyllis are simply responding with self-interest to incentives that make welfare look better than low-paying dirty work in a laundry. Such are the kinds of choices poor people face—two ugly alternatives. Who among us would show high motivation in choosing among such options? The question of human motivation at the center of the issue of poverty is whether alternatives attractive enough to draw people out of poverty can be made real for those who are poor. Will job training or child care or public employment or the three combined do the trick? If neither these nor any other positive alternatives will make a difference for most of the poor, then we are left with a negative cycle of punishment and coercion. None of what we know of psychology should lead us to believe that punishment will work better than reward to motivate people. To use the language of our theology of freedom and community, positive lures work best in leading people to be productive. Yet, most Americans are in a mood to punish.

Can those who are not poor approach the issue of poverty more positively; can we rise above simple self-interest? Poverty is such an explosive issue for most Americans precisely because it brings into question our own motivation. The working class particularly asks why they should work so hard to make a living for their families at jobs they may not like very much, when others do not work and still get by. These attitudes are usually accompanied by extremely exaggerated ideas of just how easy life is on welfare. They get stronger when, as in recent years, wages for average workers are stagnant. One alternative is to preach against the greed of most Americans, an alternative that may be appropriate for those who prosper at the expense of others. However, based upon our theology of freedom and community the better alternative would be to appeal to the long-term self-interest we all share in ending poverty.

To be very specific, the United States now finds itself in an extremely competitive world economy. Much of that competition is based upon having an educated work force from the top to the bottom of the productive process. The United States has great universities turning out highly educated graduates able to take their place at the top. However, our competitors are doing much better at the bottom, educating average workers. The key reason is poverty. We have separated the poor and nonpoor, and we are miseducating most poor children. As adults, these poor children are crowding our prisons and welfare rolls, at an immense price to us all, rather than taking their place as productive workers in the economy. If we are to move ahead, all of us, we must solve this problem of poverty. If not, we shall find it difficult to compete in the world economy, and we shall decline economically. If this description is accurate, it is in the self-interest of all Americans to deal with poverty.

HOPE

Which brings us to the matter of hope. The depth of poverty is to be on a treadmill, never really getting ahead permanently. Actually most people who are poor at any given time are not really poor in this sense. They are between jobs or are victims of an illness or other immediate problem. They will recover and not be poor next year. However, a larger number of the poor in recent years either stay poor over long periods of time or manage to rise just above poverty for a time only to fall back into poverty again. Add to this the deterioration of poor neighborhoods as institutions move out and violence grows, and hope begins to die. When hope begins to die, poverty reaches its lowest point and all of the rhetoric about the American dream sounds very hollow. Indeed, for human beings the loss of hope is the final indignity of poverty.

In our time this loss of hope in poor communities is mirrored in society at large. More and more Americans who are not poor themselves agree with all of the authors we have read that poverty is a critical, even tragic, problem in our society. They have heard the statistics and have seen the victims of poverty on television and even feel great sympathy for them and immense gratitude for not being poor themselves. What they have not been convinced of is that there is anything that could be done about poverty that would make much difference. It has become a common, if not well-grounded, belief that we tried to end poverty back in the sixties and failed. This negativeness is made worse by the recognition that our economy was growing rapidly in the sixties, whereas it is relatively stagnant now. What reason do we have to believe that we can do any better now?

Part of the threat to hope is this general sense of the loss of possibility or despair. While our theology of freedom and community surely recognizes the limits that inheritance imposes upon us, in every moment there is the possibility of creative change if we respond to the lure of God in that moment. Moments add up to real change and thus to hope. Another part of the threat to hope is more specific, whether there are real possibilities about which to hope. We turn now to the specifics of welfare policy in search of some real possibilities for positive change, but we will need to return again to the more general problem of whether meaningful action is possible.

CHAPTER ELEVEN

THE WELFARE REFORM WARS: DANIEL PATRICK MOYNIHAN AND BEYOND

From the War on Poverty through various attempts to reform welfare and the Reagan revolution up to the present day, there is one constant in welfare policy in the United States—Daniel Patrick Moynihan. As a young specialist on urban issues who had been active in the Kennedy campaign of 1960, Moynihan found himself working in the Department of Labor of the new administration. He quickly rose to assistant secretary for policy planning and research, in which capacity he served on the committee that designed the War on Poverty.

In his reflections on that process, he strongly criticized the emphasis upon community action that became the centerpiece of the program. He argued instead that the stress should be on employment and on the support systems such as education, job training, and day care necessary to put people to work. Upon reflection he recognized that such an employment strategy was simply more expensive than Lyndon Johnson could buy at the same time that he was increasing the war effort in Vietnam.[1]

None of this made Moynihan famous; a white paper to President Johnson of which he was the lead author did. Indeed that white paper (a summary of what is known about a given subject) on the black family became known as the Moynihan report. In it Moynihan argued that a primary cause of poverty and its related problems among black Americans was the instability of the black family. While Moynihan attributed this family instability to generations of discrimination, critics attacked him for blaming the victims rather than advocating changes in the social and economic systems.[2] That oversimplifies a basic difference in perspective between Moynihan and his critics. These two events made clear that two basic social institutions—work and family—and one basic principle—social integration—are the marks of Moynihan's approach to poverty policy.

For Moynihan the most fundamental goal of all social policy is to help people participate in the mainstream of our society. His basic principle is integrating people into society. He believes that the basic institutions of work and family do just that.[3] When functioning well, families not only support and nurture children personally but also teach them the basic values of the society. When functioning well, work not only provides money but also a sense of responsibility and achievement. Taken together, good families and good work provide us with a secure place in the world and a sense of meaning and purpose. They also make unnecessary any significant intervention by government as the representative of the broader society. Rather, the society functions smoothly, and individuals are integrated into it quite easily. This is what Moynihan seeks to encourage with welfare policy.

Moynihan left the Johnson administration in 1965 to run for local office in New York City. When he lost, he moved on to become a professor at Harvard University. During the following four years he wrote of his experience with the War on Poverty and wrote and edited works on poverty and urban policy.[4]

In the process he became known as a neo-conservative, in part because of his fundamental disagreement with people like Piven. He sought and seeks social change that would integrate people into the mainstream. Piven wanted and wants social change that would change the basic nature of the mainstream. In practice, this meant Moynihan wanted an employment strategy that would integrate the poor into the economic system to be at the center of the War on Poverty and opposed the Community Action Program because he felt it provoked division and discord with little positive result. Piven was closely associated with Community Action as a way to focus the rightful demands of the poor for basic social change.[5]

THE FAMILY ASSISTANCE PLAN

In 1969, Moynihan joined the new Nixon administration as its leading policy planner for urban issues. In that capacity, he took the lead in designing the Family Assistance Plan (FAP), Nixon's welfare reform proposal.[6] FAP was essentially a negative income tax moderated to fit into the realities of the federal and state welfare systems. The conservative Republican roots of the negative income tax made it a logical jumping-off point for the new administration. A major struggle developed between Moynihan as an advocate of the proposal and Arthur Burns, a conservative economic advisor who preferred a work training and referral option. Richard Nixon asked Secretary of Labor George Schultz to settle the issue. As a former professor with Milton Friedman at the University of Chicago, Schultz was inclined toward a negative income tax. His solution retained Moynihan's ideas but added more work incentives and job training to respond to Burns, thus expanding the scope and cost of the entire proposal.[7]

A table for the original FAP proposal like the one we used to understand Friedman's negative income tax proposal would look like this:

Earned Income	Government Benefit	Total Income
$0	$ 1,500	$ 1,500
1,000	1,000	2,000
2,000	500	2,500
3,000	0	3,000

Schultz quite rightly noted that it costs money to go to work (transportation, clothes, lunches, etc.) and argued that the program should recognize that, if it wanted to move people from welfare to work. He settled on a figure of $60/month ($720/year) to cover these work-related expenses and added $100 to the basic benefit. A table expressing this change follows:

Earned Income	Government Benefit	Total Income
$0	1,600	1,600
720	1,600	2,320
1,000	1,460	2,460
2,000	960	2,960
3,000	460	3,460
3,920	0	3,920

In order to be sure that no current benefits would be cut, states would have been required to pay the difference between FAP and the then-current benefit levels in each state. Unlike Friedman, FAP also assumed the continuation of other federal programs for the poor—food stamps, medical benefits, public housing, etc. To support family life, FAP required the states to include two-parent families in the program.[8]

Moynihan defended the Family Assistance Program in just the terms we would expect. He contended that it would contribute to the public order by encouraging people to work and to remain together as families. This fits with the fact that FAP was developed in the aftermath of the major civil disorders of the late sixties and Nixon had promised law and order. However, Moynihan's position was entirely consistent over time: family and work are essential to social integration. To his disappointment, however, FAP failed to get majority support. By Moynihan's account conservatives considered it too generous because it would have included the working poor and expanded benefits. This he expected. What he found more disappointing was that liberals, in and out of Congress, refused to support a significant step toward a good national policy because it did not go far enough. By his account the radicals, typified by the National Welfare Rights Organization, shamed the liberals into opposing a program that cut no benefits and expanded many, just because the benefits were not raised as much as they wanted.[9]

As FAP began to falter, a Moynihan memo to Nixon advising benign neglect of the issue of race was leaked to the press. Moynihan insisted that his advice was to support programs of assistance to all but particularly helpful to black Americans (such as FAP) instead of programs specifically focused on race. As in the case of the earlier Moynihan report, he was labeled as anti-black because of this memo. Under this cloud, he left the administration and returned to Harvard. Three years later Nixon appointed him ambassador to India and two years after that he became ambassador to the United Nations, where he made a name for himself by attacking the Soviets and defending the United States. Finally in 1976, he resigned and soon after ran for and won a Senate seat from New York; he has been in the Senate since. In that capacity he now reigns as the national legislative expert on welfare legislation in the United States.

RECENT DEVELOPMENTS

More recently, Moynihan led a much less grand effort to reform the welfare system in 1987–88.[10] As should be no surprise, one main target of this reform was to support and even require parental responsibility. It included tough new efforts to enforce child support from absent parents and to make it easier to track them down. On the other hand it required states to include families with two unemployed parents in the AFDC program; about half of the states had not done so. As we should expect, the legislation also sought to encourage and enforce work. Able-bodied recipients without child care responsibilities were required to work for the benefits. Women of younger children were also required to work and day care standards were relaxed. Finally, states were freed to propose programs for moving people from welfare to work.[11]

States have responded in various ways, depending upon the leadership and political climate in each state. Most, including Arkansas under Bill Clinton, have developed programs that try to use positive supports such as education, job training, child care, and extended health benefits to encourage recipients to get jobs. Other states have taken an approach much like that proposed by Lawrence Mead, in which they have tried to enforce certain behavior. For instance, Wisconsin has changed the law so that recipients whose children drop out of school or who become pregnant will pay a financial price in reduced benefits. The choice between these two options is often forced by budget concerns but is at least in part a question of whether legislators believe people are best motivated by positive rewards or negative punishments.

This legislation and the debate surrounding it illustrate well the shift in the ethical terms of the welfare debate during the last three decades when Moynihan has been a key actor. Back in the sixties, partially growing out of the experience of the Civil Rights Movement, the entire discussion of welfare centered on freedom. Those on the right, like Milton Friedman, argued for a negative income tax on the grounds that it would extend individual freedom. Those on the left, like the National Welfare Rights Organization, argued for the right to a guaranteed income for all Americans to assure their freedom. Those in between often got caught in the crossfire, as Moynihan believed the FAP did, but it was a conflict over what was necessary for people to be free.

In the nineties the terms of the debate have shifted to various visions of community. Mead and Wisconsin welfare law seek to enforce community standards of behavior upon people who deviate from them. Other states seek to use positive rewards to move people into the mainstream of the economy. Moynihan introduced and passed legislation that mixes some positive rewards and some negative punishments aimed at supporting the basic institutions of work and family. All share the goal of building community; for them the central ethical question is just what sort of community is good and possible. Sooner or later, good welfare policy must address issues of both freedom and community. Just what does our theology and its implications for the five key ethical questions have to say about our present debate over welfare policy and where it should head? In order to keep this discussion as specific as possible, I shall refer from time to time to the four positions we analyzed earlier. However, the primary purpose of what follows is to find an adequate policy position based upon our theology.

INDIVIDUALITY

As we have already noted, our theology of freedom and community recognizes self-determination as a fundamental necessity for people to be full human beings. Yet, this self-determination takes place between a powerful past and possible futures. We are not free to do whatever we choose, but we can make real choices. What does this understanding of self-determination have to say about welfare policy? One reality we must recognize as we begin to answer that question is that in this society employment is the most widely accepted way of establishing self-determination. Our theology supports this reality inasmuch as our work is one primary way in which we exercise our capacity to make choices and to shape the flow of events, one way we contribute back to the community. By working we gain a sense of having made our own way in the world, which is so essential to our sense of being actors as well as being acted upon. Perhaps this is why most of us believe that we should work, and all of our authors advocated work in their various ways. Some persons may find it physically or mentally difficult to be employed. Others may carry responsibilities for the care of children or other dependents that make it hard to be employed. Yet, increasingly we recognize that it is good that people who can work have jobs and that if possible they should receive some pay as our socially recognized way of saying that their jobs have value. Surely we recognize that work has value beyond being paid and that we are not paid for some of our most important work. Still, in the real world people who are never paid for their work have trouble being valued or valuing themselves for it.

Charles Murray argues for the elimination of all federal welfare programs, leaving only those private and local charity efforts that people are willing to support with their contributions or local taxes. He assumes that these local programs will be much, much smaller and a lot tougher than current programs. He seeks these changes in order to allow the market to foster, or even force, self-sufficiency in poor people. If Harold and Phyllis can get no welfare they will have to take care of themselves.[12] He is convinced that individuals are best able to take responsibility for themselves if they are not dependent on others. Milton Friedman defends a negative income tax on the same ethical grounds. The difference is that he does not believe that the general public will agree to Murray's radical proposal to eliminate all assistance.[13] Based upon our theological understanding of self-determination, we *should* not agree to do so. Murray simply does not pay enough attention to how much we are shaped by our place in the world, a world that distributes opportunities and resources very unequally.

If there are going to be some welfare benefits, Friedman believes they should be given in the form of a negative income tax. This would eliminate many of the bureaucratic controls over recipients that are a part of the present system. The ethical strength of this position is that it seeks to recognize the self-determination of the poor. Most Americans are not willing to do this. The reason we have food stamps and medical benefits and housing grants is because we do not trust poor people with money. We can blame this on politicians or government bureaucrats, but it is in fact their attempt to respond to the views of the vast majority of voters. We say that we want the poor to be independent but do not trust them to act independently.

If we are to further self-determination as we have described it based on our theology, some version of a negative income tax seems like an appropriate means of distributing a minimum national benefit. This leaves open the question of the level of the benefits, the amount of the work incentive, or the precise mechanism to be used. As I have already suggested, these are huge loose ends, which have pulled earlier reform efforts apart. How they are tied up will make any particular welfare proposals much more or less acceptable. For instance, a minimum benefit of less than the official poverty level is morally indefensible in a society as affluent as ours.

COMMUNITY

A bigger question may be whether the community has satisfied its responsibility to poor people by sending them a check. Friedman believes so and would eliminate all other programs that assist the poor. One of the main virtues of a negative income tax is that it interferes least with the market. The trouble is that it is not hard to imagine a negative income tax merely subsidizing low-wage work. This would leave a group of people stuck in low-paying jobs with little chance of ever moving up to better ones. The negative income tax may have raised them a little bit above the official poverty level, appearing to solve the problem of poverty. Yet, they would be not much better off personally and no fuller participants in the wider society than they were when they were officially poor. This is why we must add various programs to help them into a job and up the ladder of advancement.

This brings us to the question of just what the community should do to support employment. The most basic assumption of Mead's policy proposals for requiring poor people to work is that poor people are responsible for their poverty so it is appropriate to force them to change their behavior. This seems to be a basic inconsistency in Mead's position. He stresses the ways in which the community shapes individual behavior, and yet he holds the poor responsible as individuals and proposes no significant changes in society. To be specific, we are in an economy that increasingly requires education in order for people to get jobs that pay enough to support a family. Yet, a significant portion of our population is not getting a good education because of the huge difference in quality among our schools. This is not some sociological theory. All Americans know it, and (if they have the money) most parents move to school districts that will increase the chances of success for their children. We could explore other examples of basic inequalities that produce very different odds of success for different Americans. How can we ignore these realities of our social order and blame the individuals affected? Our theology certainly cannot justify doing so.

The standard positive alternatives for work assistance are job training or direct job creation. In a rapidly changing economy, the problem with both is that government-operated programs tend to lack the flexibility necessary to keep current. For instance, government job training programs often train people for jobs of the past on outdated equipment. At the same time, workers who may change jobs a number of times during their lifetimes need basic education. The best solution seems to be for government to take responsibility for basic education primarily by contracting with training centers. The actual skills necessary in particular jobs are best developed on that job with the equipment actually used to do it. This training can be supported when necessary by tax credits to the employer. This has been the basic direction of job training policy in recent years.

Direct government job creation is a more difficult issue. If there is an important public need not being met, which could be done by the unemployed, job creation makes real sense. However, too often job creation programs have provided short-term jobs that pay little and offer no advancement over time. Most of our summer jobs programs have fallen into this category. If anything, this sort of job creation may just act as a substitute for the basic education and job training that must occur. At the same time, we would do better to fund our schools and local governments adequately enough so that they can afford assistant teachers, road crews, housing rehabilitation, and such on a long-term basis. Then, we should provide the basic education and training that will help the poor get jobs and advance in them. Short-term, make-work jobs with no future may simply freeze people in jobs vulnerable to the next round of budget cuts. This is not what our theology means by full participation in the community.

Any efforts to deal with poverty that take the role of the community seriously will include more than income maintenance. It will add basic education and job training. To do less is to raise serious doubts about whether this society does in fact believe that people should work if they are able. If the poor are to be full participants in the community, they must not be segregated in second-class jobs, public or private. Whatever the public role in making full employment at adequate wages a reality, it is finally justified by our recognition that we all share a world made richer as more of us are more able to contribute creatively to it.

171

WORTH

Murray claims that the best way to respect the poor is to eliminate welfare. Then we can respect those poor persons who manage to keep their heads above water. This is only a debating point. In spite of our attachment to stories about the courageous poor, those who are not poor tend to look down on all poor people as failures.[14] This ignores the importance of the social context, which is a central aspect of our theology. Mead shares the same view of the worth of poor people, but he wants government to insist that people behave in certain ways in order to reinforce society's values. What this comes to is an attempt to define the worth of recipients in terms of conformity to society's moral standards.[15] This is clearly inconsistent with the view of worth we have developed out of our understanding of the human condition. If productive activity (usually through work) helps people develop a sense of worth and if we agree that healthy families are essential to the development of healthy children, then the community should seek to reinforce the value of work and family. The problem is Mead's attempt to *compel* behavior consistent with the values of work and family. This is contrary to the pluralistic kind of community consistent with our theology of freedom and community.

Actually, Mead's proposals for using welfare policy to force people to behave in a way consistent with the mainstream values of the society assumes quite a lot. First, it assumes that we agree on those values and that they are not in conflict with one another. For instance, we no doubt agree at a very general level that it is good for able-bodied persons to work. However, those who are directly affected by the changes in AFDC policy that Mead proposes are almost all mothers with young children. Americans are deeply ambiguous and divided about whether the mother of a three-year-old should be working outside of the home. One traditional American value, deeply held, is work; another American value, just as deeply held, is family. Everyday life consists in the trade-off and balance among such values, which each of us individually must figure out for ourselves.[16] However, the authoritative enforcement by government of one of these values at the expense of another requires that the entire society agree pretty specifically on the relative importance of each value or that some of us force others to accept our view of what is proper. This is precisely why libertarian conservatives prefer to keep government out of these issues. Our theology would stress persuasion and pluralism over the compulsion and conformity that Mead's position requires.

A related assumption Mead makes is that it is possible to enforce the regulations effectively and fairly. To do so, active and competent bureaucrats will have to get pretty deeply involved in the lives of the recipients. They will need to gather information about school attendance, pregnancy and birth, work effort, employer practices, or the quality of day care. They will have to decide whether students have dropped out of school, children have been born, people are able to work, jobs are appropriate and administered properly, or day care is available and adequate. In each case bureaucrats must decide for and about people. For libertarians, conservative and liberal, this paternalism is highly suspect in principle; it is also very difficult in practice. Welfare bureaucracies are notorious for staff turnover and burnout; it turns out that enforcing welfare rules is not a pleasant or rewarding job. Given these realities, carrying out our urge to regulate the behavior of people is both more dangerous and more difficult than we may expect.[17] It almost certainly would require a larger and better-paid bureaucracy than we have now.

Instead of this public welfare bureaucracy whose job it is to enforce moral values shared by society at large, Schorr proposes supportive social services. Schorr's policy proposals are not particularly new. The Kennedy administration's primary welfare changes were an expansion in social services to assist recipients to move to work. We Americans tend to prefer helping individuals (even with government programs), to changing social structures, and much of what Schorr proposes seems to make real sense. Given our theology of freedom and community, we must offer some cautions. For example, my wife teaches kindergarten in a school that includes many low-income children. Her classroom mixes many of the latest in educational techniques with a loving, supportive, joyful atmosphere. I think Schorr would include it among her programs that work. However, those children go home to neighborhoods and peers who may lead them in destructive directions and to parents who are so burdened with the daily struggle to survive that they have far too little left to give to their kids. Nothing my wife does in her classroom can change those realities; only good jobs, safe neighborhoods, and supportive community institutions will. The best in social services may have little effect without social change.

Two other problems directly related to a social service strategy must also be kept in mind. Social services that serve primarily or exclusively poor people are almost inevitably second-rate compared to those that serve those who are not poor. Hospitals, schools, mental health programs, parks, or whatever else we can name that separate by income nearly always provide services of different quality.[18] The solution is simple but controversial because it challenges the privileges of those who are not poor. Our medical system, mental health services, schools, parks, or other basic services should be made universally available if we are to be sure of their quality. We who are not poor have the power to force the providers of those services to maintain good quality if they serve us. If they serve only the poor, that is unlikely.

Second, regardless of how hard service providers try, most social services for the poor are by nature paternalistic. Someone with skills, usually being paid reasonably well, is providing help to someone in need with much less income. This is critical to the very nature of the services. If the person sending out welfare checks thinks recipients are lazy and undeserving, it makes little difference; the check still cashes. However, if the doctor treating your child or the teacher teaching her does not think she is of value, that attitude will likely handicap their work.[19] Human services are relationships among persons; their success depends upon mutual respect. Doctors, teachers, and other professionals who are callous, cynical, or burned out are probably ineffective. This is a danger that the service providers always must guard against and does raise the question of whether a good job or adequate income is not the most important social service our society can provide its members.[20]

Recognizing all of these limitations upon a social service strategy, Schorr makes a solid case for their value in many situations, especially where they can play a preventive role. Every effort should be made to integrate the poor into programs that serve broader populations and to fight the tendency to paternalism. Most of all, they must never be seen as a substitute for full employment or an adequate benefit for those not employed.

The caution this whole discussion offers to all of us, poor and not poor alike, is to rethink our own sense of worth. Too often the battles over welfare deteriorate into a struggle over whether I am going to get mine and keep it or have it taxed away to help others. These views are often expressed with the greatest anger by those who themselves are not all that well off (especially in an economy that is not growing), but they are shared by many who are much better off. What does this have to say about our sense of what we ourselves are worth? Is our worth decided by our income? Murray is quick to conclude that being well off is not as important as being independent. Are we as willing to conclude that living in a society with much less poverty is important enough to our own sense of worth to give up some of our income? Our theology of the human condition implies that our worth will be enhanced by living in a community where people are able to contribute. Poverty prevents that. By respecting the inherent worth of others, we also affirm that our own human worth cannot be reduced to merely income or wealth.

MOTIVATION

All of the experts on poverty and welfare we have discussed and nearly all Americans agree that a significant number of the people presently receiving welfare would be better off working. But how? The basic problem is that a welfare grant that comes anywhere close to providing an adequate minimum income for a family is competitive with a low-wage job. If we recognize that there are costs, both financial (clothes, transportation, day care, loss of health insurance, etc.) and human (relationship with child, time for household work, etc.), to going to work, many people are going to choose welfare. If we recognize that the vast majority of welfare recipients are mothers on their own with children, the choice of going to work is made even more difficult. Why would any mother choose to work a long day at a hard job and then come home to care for children, pay bills, shop, cook, and clean if she is no better off for doing so than if she stayed home full time? We can discuss values all we want, but with the current set of incentives we are asking many mothers with children, the majority of AFDC recipients, for heroic commitment to the work ethic.

Murray's solution is simple enough: eliminate the welfare option. Left with no alternative but the low-wage job, people will have to take it. If men realize that government will not feed their children, they will have to step up to their responsibility to do so. For Murray, the real world is a harsh reality from which people cannot be protected without being robbed of their independence.[21] Of course if jobs that pay enough to support a family are really not available or a number of parents decide to leave their families rather than support their children, then children will suffer. Remember, children make up the majority of welfare recipients. Murray says that in such cases private and local charities will step in to help. However, past experience indicates that their efforts will be neither large enough nor comprehensive enough. Children and their parents will suffer. Murray is confident that these possibilities will motivate people, but it seems just as likely that they will overwhelm and depress them.

Mead simply does not believe that it is possible to make low-wage jobs attractive to people and doubts that we are willing to let their children suffer. The solution, then, is to require poor people to work. This turns welfare bureaucrats into enforcers and enemies of recipients. And so the game begins. Welfare workers try to catch the cheaters, and recipients figure out how to escape regulation as much as possible. Psychologists suggest that when we punish people, we have no way of knowing how they will respond. Some may work hard. Others will work only as much as they are forced to do. Will such compulsion move people on to productive employment with a future of promotion and adequate pay or keep them in a game of cat and mouse with welfare regulations?

Schorr clearly seems on the right path in suggesting that people respond better to positive possibilities than to punishment. Various states have used the flexibility of the Moynihan reforms of 1988 to devise programs that bring together education, job training, day care, and extended health benefits to make it possible for people to move into good jobs. This is much more consistent with the theology we have developed than what Murray and Mead propose. The question that remains is the one we have consistently raised of Schorr. Is our economy producing the good jobs into which these former recipients can move? If not, they may be worse off financially when they work, even after they get help with education, job training, day care, and health benefits. Positive motivation requires both supportive services and a social context that provides opportunity.

Now, what would cause taxpayers to support the added expense of positive motivations? Reality might, if our theology of the human condition is correct. As long as we think that the interests of the poor and of those who are not poor are at odds, most of us who are not poor will oppose welfare. We can condemn this morally; we should be concerned about our fellow human beings. However, in an economy where the wages of the middle-income group are stagnant or declining, it is unlikely that most people will agree to give up more of their income for others. Murray and Mead speak to the interests of those who are not poor, and Piven advocates the interests of the poor, but they all share the view that welfare generates a conflict of interests. No wonder the present system is so unpopular with the public, and calls forth some kind of reform program from any serious political candidate.

But are the interests of the poor and those who are not poor finally at odds? Not if our theology of the human condition is true. Poor children growing up in our society run a high risk of not being educated well enough to get a good job. In an economy that needs a productive work force, that represents a loss of economic growth for us all. This is particularly true in a global economy where our primary competitors do not have the same income disparities and their connected problems. But the story does not end there. Poor children who do not get education and jobs do not disappear. They become young adults who get in trouble with the law and who have children we will not let starve. Poverty increases, welfare costs go up, and the demand for prison beds explodes. These too are economic costs for the entire society.[22] An economy that is growing and schools that are educating children well will be good for those who are not poor as well as those who are. On sheer economic grounds, it is in the interest of all for poor children to become productive adults. This is all entirely consistent with our theology of human freedom and community, which recognizes that we incorporate into ourselves the world that we share with others.

However, we share more than an economy. Those who are not poor, especially those nearly so, live in the same neighborhoods and send their children to the same schools as the poor. Others have moved away from poverty to supposedly safe neighborhoods, often at great cost to themselves. In recent years this geographic division is being driven increasingly by fear.[23] Politicians play on these fears or try to ignore them because they are too powerful to overcome. We all pay a price for this division and fear in a lost sense of shared purpose and in stunted human relationships. If, as we have suggested, we become who we are out of our relationships to others and the community we share, we simply cannot become our best in such a society. We cannot separate out our individual interests and seek our own at the expense of others. Our destinies are much too intricately intertwined for us to get ahead at the expense of others in the long run. This is a central lesson of our theology of human freedom and community. In the meantime, however, many will try to do so if this reality does not become clear to them.

I did not include a section on hope in this chapter because it is important enough to require a whole chapter of its own. That chapter follows.

CHAPTER TWELVE

WHERE DO WE GO FROM HERE?
BILL CLINTON AND BEYOND

In 1967 the last book by Martin Luther King, Jr., to appear while he was alive—*Where Do We Go from Here: Chaos or Community?*—was published.[1] By turning Dr. King into a saint, we often ignore his important role as a social critic and politician. Much of his last book was dedicated to explaining his response to black power and white backlash. However, near the end of the book, when he turned to public policy, the issue he separated out for special attention was poverty.[2] At the time of his death, Martin Luther King, Jr., was deeply involved in organizing the Poor People's Campaign to call for jobs or income for all Americans. Some have criticized civil rights leaders like King for straying away from their basic purposes when they take up poverty.[3] However, as long as African Americans are three times more likely to be poor, as long as half of their children are poor, and as long as the face most Americans see when they think of a welfare recipient is black, poverty will remain a civil rights issue.

Several other lessons are to be learned from the fact that King had targeted this issue for action twenty-five years ago. We Americans tend to think that there are simple solutions to problems if smart people with good intentions figure out what needs to be done and do it.[4] On the contrary, if a problem is in fact an issue in our social life that raises basic questions about how our society should be organized and about the very meaning of our lives, quick and simple solutions elude us. Poverty is such an issue. It is unlikely that in this last chapter I will be able to propose a simple set of policy options that will find broad political support and soon end poverty any more than Dr. King did.

HOPE

In our earlier discussion of hope, I suggested that the two reasons for hope based upon our theology of human freedom and community were the fundamental value of the ideal sought and the potential contribution to long-term positive change. Recognizing that the issue was complicated and not knowing whether he would be politically successful did not stop Dr. King from proposing what he felt was just. The justice of his proposal, or ours, is the fundamental ground of our hope. Second, King liked to say that the arc of the universe is long but it bends toward justice. In other words, our current actions, even when they seem unsuccessful, may contribute to the long-term success of justice. In this light, King's proposals can be seen as one step in the long effort of addressing poverty. Let us see whether we can take another step, however much smaller.

I will describe the long-term policy goals for dealing with poverty that I believe follow from our theological and ethical analysis. Then I will suggest some immediate directions policy can take toward reaching these long-term goals. A good place to begin is by returning to the four factors I identified in the first chapter to see whether we have more to say about them now than we did at that time.

THE FOUR FACTORS

The first factor I identified was general economic growth. The positions we have analyzed does not have much to say about this topic. However, it has been a matter of general public debate, intellectual discussion, and ethical analysis for years.[5] Surely in an affluent, post-industrial economy like ours, growth does not need to take the form of more consumer goods for the vast majority of Americans. Yet, there is no evidence to suggest that it does not remain the case that a growing economy lays essential groundwork for dealing with poverty. A growing economy does not guarantee a decline in poverty, but it is hard to believe that a significant decrease in poverty will occur if the economy is stagnant. We ignore the interlocking of economic growth and poverty at our own peril.

The second factor I identified was the changing character of America's labor force. Again there is considerable controversy over whether the United States' government should attempt to help private corporations who pay high wages compete in the world market. Policies proposed include trade protection, government subsidies for research and development, and tax breaks for investments designed to keep our workers competitive.[6] Others argue that such policies merely retard the creative destruction necessary for a market economy to adjust to new competitive realities. In the long run, they insist, we must make the tough decisions necessary to compete rather than try to postpone the day of reckoning. Otherwise, we will simply become less and less competitive.[7] Again this issue ranges beyond the materials we have considered here, but cannot be ignored. What does begin to come within the scope of our analysis are programs designed to help people, young and older alike, to develop the skills necessary to earn a living in the contemporary economy. This is of both personal and social significance since one major disadvantage we face in competing in the world market is that our labor force is not as well educated or as skilled as our major competitors. In part, this involves our basic educational system, which increasingly reinforces and passes on poverty rather than helping students escape it. This topic of education reform is also beyond the scope of our detailed inquiry but cannot be ignored as a contributing force. Head Start and compensatory educational programs for low-income students can make some difference. However, in the end it is difficult to see how any real solution to educational inequality can occur without fundamental changes in how we fund education and where we live.

Basic education and job training for people beyond school age clearly does fall within the broader scope of antipoverty programs. There seems to be growing recognition that we would be more successful if we made apprenticeship education generally available for those not planning to go to college, rather than wait for people to show up on welfare rolls before we try to intervene. Our key international competitors do so already. There also is growing recognition that government should help workers whose jobs disappear make the transition to new jobs. What remains under debate is just how government should provide this assistance—conservatives like vouchers for individuals while liberals prefer comprehensive programs. Let us hope that we do not allow this ideological debate to keep us from educating our work force for good jobs. This will both allow workers to support their families and help our economy grow. While there are serious intellectual issues to be addressed in trying to act effectively in each of these first two areas, it is possible to conceive of assembling the necessary political support for such action. This is much less clear when we turn to the third factor—our social divisions.

There is, I believe, a genuine desire to overcome these divisions at an abstract level. When we become very concrete, that resolve evaporates. William Julius Wilson, the leading voice in describing these divisions, shrinks from direct confrontation with them.[8] It is, for instance, hard to see how we will ever break down these divisions as long as the poor are concentrated in certain neighborhoods. The obvious solution is to disperse the poor throughout the metropolitan areas. Theoretically, this could be done with effective use of subsidized housing. Does anyone believe that an attempt to spread low-income housing throughout suburban communities is anything but political suicide? I do not. At the same time, I find Wilson's solutions (centered on full employment) unlikely seriously to challenge our geography of division.[9]

This does not mean that some important things cannot be done. Enterprise zones with tax breaks for investing in poor neighborhoods may lure some businesses away from suburban locations. Funds for improved police protection and housing rehabilitation can make some old neighborhoods more livable. Policies governing public housing can attempt to spread out subsidized housing as much as possible within political realities and make already-built projects more livable. Government at all levels can help schools that serve poor children do a better jobs of educating children so they can be more successful in our economy. Most of all, full employment can make it possible for men and women to stay together and support their families and either move or help make their neighborhoods more livable. Whether these efforts will finally break down our social divisions remains doubtful, but they are steps forward that are worth a try.

PRINCIPLES FOR WELFARE REFORM

That brings us to the factor we have considered in great detail: public policy addressed directly at supporting and assisting the poor. We shall focus on it at great length, never forgetting that these other three factors have much to do with both whether the full dimensions of the issue of poverty are addressed and whether these direct programs are even successful. In the preceding chapter we discussed the implications for welfare policy that we drew from our theology and the full understanding of poverty we developed from it. Now, we can state some basic principles for adequate welfare reform which restate what we have learned in briefer form.

If we were to summarize our discussion of the first four ethical questions in the last chapter in terms of principles for adequate welfare reform they might come to the following:

1. Humans must be self-determining to some considerable extent if we are to be creative and contributing members of society. Some variation on a negative income tax appears to be the best policy for granting benefits to poor people while preserving their self-determination.
2. A good community should provide the support necessary for its members to contribute fully. Given our emphasis upon work in this society this means that programs which help people get the education and skills necessary to get a job or a better one are essential.
3. Human worth should not be reduced to our income or economic value rather than our potential for creative contribution to the world we share. Social services provided as broadly and well as possible, with full respect for the clients, should be available to provide the supports necessary for people to become productive human beings.
4. Most people respond best to positive incentives to creative activity rather than punishment. Programs should reward people for their efforts to advance themselves; punitive programs should be resisted.

These four principles would not be agreeable to all four of the authors we have read in detail. However, our theology of freedom and community suggests that principles such as these should guide our attempts to improve the American welfare system.

AN IDEAL SYSTEM

Starting with these principles the ideal welfare system should provide a *minimum benefit* for all Americans, which assures that they have income adequate to give them and their children the resources necessary to be active participants in our society. It is hard to see how a minimum benefit below the official poverty level can possibly do this. It seems very unlikely that such a level will be reached except through a national system since many of the states with higher levels of poverty are the very states without the revenue or political will to provide adequate benefits. We must establish a goal of a national minimum benefit, which can certainly be adjusted to local costs of living, at least at the poverty level. Some version of a negative income tax, whether or not we call it that, is the simplest and fairest way to do this. Some amount of money earned should be subject to no reduction in benefits because it truly does cost money to go to work. Above that allowance for the cost of going to work a 50 percent reduction in benefits seems about right.

In addition to money, people need *job training and full employment.* Government should provide the basic education that allows people to train for a job now and retrain for advancement or another job later. This is usually done most efficiently and with the strongest personal encouragement on the local level, often by nonprofit organizations. On the other hand, actual job training is usually best carried out by employers themselves, encouraged by some sort of tax credit if necessary. When government identifies important unmet public needs, it should create jobs to meet them. Economic policies designed to maximize employment in the general economy are essential to the success of programs that try to move people from welfare to employment.

People need *basic human services.* Insofar as possible, these services should be provided to all Americans—national health insurance, community mental health, day care, or college scholarships, for instance. This will make it much more likely that these services will be of good quality and will be politically less vulnerable. Those of us who are not poor will use our power to assure that these services are of good quality if they serve us all regardless of income. Programs specifically designed to compensate for the disadvantages of the poor must be carried out with imagination and respect for the clients. In my experience, not-for-profit agencies tend to do this better than public agencies, even if the not-for-profits are funded with government money.

People should receive *encouragement to work* if they can and should be better off economically when they do so. A system of work incentive should be available whether or not people have ever been on welfare. Notches in all other government programs should be eliminated. This could be done most simply by providing cash instead of food stamps, housing subsidies, and so on. This would also eliminate any underground markets, which recipients now use to get cash for these benefits. Whatever it takes, people should not be punished economically for working or working more. That leaves the issue that may be the toughest politically, but I believe is pretty clear in principle. Welfare policy should provide positive motivation for recipients to support their children and to go to work. Should such behavior be demanded, and failure to practice it be punished? The answer in the case of child support is yes, although poor fathers who leave their families are not likely to be able to provide much support for their children. Perhaps absent parents could be offered education and training with the requirement that a portion of their income will go automatically to support their children. Otherwise, positive incentives create automatic punishments. If it pays to work, it costs not to do so. Any punishments beyond these are more likely to hurt the children involved than to produce the desired changes in behavior.

An ideal welfare system based upon our theology of freedom and community would provide *a national minimum benefit, basic education and job training, full employment, supportive human services, and positive incentives for employment.* All of this would need to take place in the context of coming to terms with the other factors that cause poverty. What real possibilities for changes such as these in our welfare system are on the horizon? That is the question to which we now turn.

CLINTON PROPOSALS

The most likely source of change in welfare policy on the horizon is the Clinton administration. There is no better place to begin a discussion of immediate options for changes in the welfare system. In his own way, Clinton has spoken to each of the four factors we have identified as key to dealing with poverty. Economic growth was at the

185

center of his campaign for the presidency, and at the center of his analysis of the economy was his recognition of the changes in the job market discussed here. Clinton was direct but much less specific about our social divisions. He continually restated the position that we shall progress together or not at all. On the other hand, he remained distant from actual policies other than general economic growth that are designed to address social division. He was a master at doing what Wilson proposed, advocating general reforms rather than specific policies.[10]

Much less discussed is Clinton's position on welfare reform. It is a mixture of tough rhetoric and support for work effort.[11] Like all other serious contemporary politicians Clinton advocates tough enforcement of child support laws. Who can disagree, except to question just how much money that will produce for poor children? We should try. Beyond child support, Clinton's overarching position on welfare is that it is meant for temporary support until a person moves to work rather than as permanent support. This makes for good political rhetoric for a politician claiming to be a new kind of Democrat, but just what does it mean? For single adults the message is crystal clear—get a job. However, few of these people receive very much federal assistance now, and most states have already instituted tough work requirements and many have cut off or reduced dramatically General Assistance grants.[12] For able-bodied adults who have children but are not responsible for their care, the message is also very clear— get a job and support your family. For the parent who is alone with her[13] children the message is much less clear. We can only assume that Clinton will settle somewhere near where Moynihan did in the latest legislation. Mothers of very young children can stay home to care for them. When their youngest child reaches a certain age, mothers probably also will be expected to take a least a part-time job.

Despite the tough rhetoric, Clinton's proposals will go beyond just these work requirements. To make it possible for people to work, he favors providing education and job training and extending benefits (like health care) after people go to work. Moreover, he expanded the Earned Income Tax Credit, a current provision of the federal income tax, which functions as a negative income tax for the working poor. Interestingly, some of the most ardent foes of welfare are strong supporters of a tax credit for the poor who work.[14] All of these provisions seem to be good ideas. In fact, states are allowed to do most of them under current law. The real questions about these proposals themselves is just how much we will be willing to invest (to use Clinton's term) in the work provisions. They are certain to cost more than is saved in unpaid welfare benefits, at least in the short run. For instance, even relatively generous states typically cut off Medicaid after a former welfare recipient has worked for six months. Perhaps national health insurance will solve this problem, but in the meantime what is a person working at a low-wage job to do when the Medicaid ends? Even more fundamental, will the Earned Income Tax Credit be expanded enough to provide substantial work incentive, or will this prove too expensive, given the budget deficits projected?

Beyond these work provisions loom the really difficult questions about welfare reform. First among these questions is just what we think about the place of single mothers in our society. Many conservatives like Mead speak glowingly about the value of the traditional family—about the need for mothers to stay home to provide a loving and supportive environment for their children, especially when they are young. Most women, including those who work, agree. Yet the same conservatives support legislation to require poor mothers to go to work, in some states as soon as their youngest child reaches one year of age. For some of us this is a sad, but fair, compromise with reality. At a time when most women work, especially those who are near poverty who must work in order for the family to stay out of poverty, is it fair for mothers on welfare to escape this necessity?

Supporters of a work requirement for mothers often argue that it is probably best for the average disorganized young woman to get a job and better for her children to be in quality day care. Critics would point out that most of the young women involved can only get low-paying jobs that provide less of a sense of purpose and responsibility than being a good parent.[15] They would point out that current welfare regulations encourage these young women to find a babysitter of questionable qualifications rather than quality day care in order to save money. They paint the picture of a mother frantically rushing her child to a babysitter who is herself a poor mother with no education credentials or to a low-cost day care center whose staff turns over every three or four months. Some of the children are abused or neglected; others simply never form stable relationships with adults. After work the mother picks up her children and then must carry the whole load of the household—cooking, cleaning, washing, and read-

187

ing books to the children and playing with them. Perhaps the key lesson to be learned is that families, and especially single mothers, need access to quality day care. We can decry the disappearance of the traditional family if we want, but the children of most of today's families that have both parents working or a single parent working need loving and stimulating care while their parents work. In any event, the issue of forcing single parents, which is almost always women, with young children to work is not simple and should be settled in a way that places priority upon the welfare of the children involved.[16]

Besides the work incentives and requirements issues, there remains the apparently simple question of how much the basic welfare grant should be. Behind this question lie some realities of the geography of poverty in the United States. Poverty is concentrated in inner cities and in rural areas and especially in Southern states. For the reasons we discussed earlier, our welfare system has developed in a way that puts the primary decisions about the level of benefits at the state and local level. The predictable result is that poor states and localities provide low benefits, and so the benefits are lowest precisely where the needs are most stark. The solution seems obvious enough, a national minimum benefit adjusted for regional differences in the cost of living.

Past attempts at welfare reform have been lost over this very question. Nixon and Carter both attempted to establish such a national minimum. Each chose a number that conservatives (especially Southerners) considered too high and liberals (especially Northerners) considered too low. In fact, the argument can be made that a national minimum grant would help both poor and affluent areas. It would reduce any incentive for people to move to high-benefits states. It might also push up wages in poorer areas, making them less attractive to businesses migrating from higher-wage areas. Clearly it would pump a lot of money into the poorer areas of the country. Both Nixon and Carter attempted to solve this problem by allowing states and localities to set benefits at a level higher than the minimum and even continuing to pay half of the benefits above the minimum. The basic number remained the subject of angry debate and doomed reform. No wonder Clinton would rather talk about the Earned Income Tax Credit and about work incentives. Sooner or later, however, we will have to face this question of a disparity in the level of benefits. We can hope it will be easier to do so if the economy improves and work incentives have been strengthened.

Finally, there will be considerable pressure to enact various new welfare provisions that try to force recipients to behave in particular ways and punish them if they do not. They will be particularly attractive to the administration of a president who stresses responsibility as Clinton does. The key will be whether Clinton will provide positive incentives for such responsibility or try to coerce it. In today's political climate some may be inevitable. Too much dependence on coercion will undermine the value of the overall proposal. In summary, Clinton's proposals for work incentives are steps in the right direction, his neglect of basic benefit levels is understandable but regrettable, and whether he gives in to pressure to punish poor people is yet to be seen.

As this book goes to press at the beginning of 1994, it is not clear just what form the final proposal for welfare reform from the Clinton administration will take. I am reluctant to respond to the preliminary recommendations of the study group that have been leaked to the press because they may not survive presidential review. In any event, the specific provisions of the final proposal are likely to be a mixture of positive and negative elements when judged by the principles I have developed. For good or ill, the legislative process also will produce some alternative possibilities. Hopefully, the preceding analysis will help us understand what is at stake and reach some judgments about which parts of the administration's proposals and the legislative alternatives deserve our support and which ones we should oppose.

BRINGING THE ACTION BACK HOME

The election of Bill Clinton to the presidency is an interesting lesson in how to think about social change. Clinton has clear connections to the Children's Defense Fund, the strongest voice for the poor within the political process just now.[17] He seems personally to share many of their policy goals for what he calls investing in our children. If the key to social change is one powerful political figure who sees an issue in the right way, the agenda of the Children's Defense Fund should be enacted during the Clinton presidency. Indeed, the first budget submitted by the Clinton administration included much of what the Children's Defense Fund wanted.

As that budget reached Congress, and particularly the United States Senate, changes began to occur. Some taxes were eliminated and some expenditures cut. Whether the new programs the Children's Defense Fund wanted remained or were cut depended in part upon the power and influence of the president. They never got this far under previous presidents. However, it is just as important to have a voluntary association such as the Children's Defense Fund lobbying Congress directly and indirectly through the contacts of its constituency with Congress. Add to this the efforts of other similar groups who agree with the Children's Defense Fund on these programs and the makings of a successful political effort emerges. In sum, the future of America's children is too important to leave in the hands of one individual, even the president of the United States.

What this represents here is a particular view of how democracy overcomes steam, of how social change can occur in democracy. It brings the responsibility for positive social change, for making history, right back home. A person or group of persons identify an issue in our public life which must be addressed, in this case grinding poverty for far too many of our children. She or they find others who share their passion and analysis and they learn to articulate that issue so that it involves some deep public purpose, in this case the future of our children. They educate themselves about the specifics of the issue and develop a plan of attack upon it. They learn to describe the issue in a way that convinces more and more people that it is important for them to join in the effort, in this case because it threatens the survival and flourishing of the whole society. On the basis of this deep public purpose, clear analysis, and broad public interest, they seek to win a majority vote of elected officials or the electorate itself.[18]

The following extended quotation from Marian Wright Edelman embodies this view of social change:

> When the new century dawns with new global economic and military challenges, America will be ready to compete economically and lead morally only if we
>
> 1. stop cheating and neglecting our children for selfish, short-sighted, personal, and political gain;
> 2. stop clinging to our racial past and recognize that America's ideals, future,

and fate are as inextricably intertwined with the fate of its poor and nonwhite children as with its privileged and white ones;

3. love our children more than we fear each other and our perceived or real external enemies;

4. acquire the discipline to invest preventively and systematically in all of our children *now* in order to reap a better trained work force and more stable future *tomorrow;*

5. curb the desires of the overprivileged so that the survival needs of the less privileged may be met, and spend less on weapons of death and more on lifelines of constructive development for our citizens;

6. set clear, national, state, city, community, and personal goals for child survival and development, and invest whatever leadership, commitment, time, money, and sustained effort are needed to achieve them;

7. struggle to begin to live our lives in less selfish and more purposeful ways, redefining success by national and international character and service rather than by national consumption and the superficial barriers of race and class. The mounting crisis of our children and families is a rebuke to everything America professes to be. While the cost of repairing our crumbling national foundation will be expensive in more ways than one, the cost of not repairing it, or patching it cosmetically, may be fatal.[19]

In the very next sentence Edelman says: "The place to begin is in ourselves. Care."[20] I teach undergraduate college students courses on social issues. If I am not careful, I teach them about the complexities and depth of an issue so well that their main conclusion is that little old me cannot do very much about this issue. And they are right. Little old me acting alone can do very little about most of the significant issues in this world we share. A voluntary association like the Children's Defense Fund depends for its success on persuading enough persons to care enough to work together to address an issue. When it works, this is democracy at its best. Our responsibility in a democracy is to try to make it work more often. It is also our hope.

THE MORAL ISSUES REMAIN

The limited possibilities for full welfare reform in the present political climate returns us to basics. The fact that the welfare expenditures that are most controversial (Aid to Families with Dependent Children and General Assistance) actually involve fairly small amounts of money compared to other entitlements (such as Social Security or Medicare or even Food Stamps or Medicaid) is a big clue that AFDC and GA hit nerves in our national psyche. They challenge our basic social values.

Those who get so angry about welfare see it not just as politically inept or administratively sloppy programs but as a challenge to the meaning of their own life. They are working hard at a job that they may not like that much and are afraid of losing. They and their spouses are both working when they think one of them should be home with the kids. They are single parents who work jobs outside their homes and then come home to all of the household work. What is the meaning of the lives they are giving to these struggles if it appears others can just sit home and collect government benefits? Their understanding of what life is really like on welfare may not be accurate. It actually may be a cycle of struggle and despair even more stark than that of those who work each day. That does not change how so many of those who attack welfare feel.

Poverty and welfare is not finally a factual or political or administrative issue; it is a moral and religious one. It has to do with what we believe at a deep level about individuality and community and human worth and motivation and with whether we will lead with our fears or with our hopes. Our welfare system is a mess not because our politicians have not been responsive to our views but because they have reflected our ethical confusion so very well.

In response to this religious challenge, I have offered a theology of freedom and community that understands human beings as actors within the flow of events able to practice democracy in the face of powerful steam. On the basis of this theology we have come to see poverty as a full human tragedy for all of us—an injustice that raises the most basic questions about the meaning and value of our very lives. This has enlightened our thinking about welfare and provided grounds for evaluating current policy options.

However, what is finally at stake in this issue of poverty is our very hearts and souls. Will we who are not poor strike out in anger at the poor in whose faces we see our own fears of what we are or might become? Or will we join in an effort to bring our society together in the common enterprise of improving the lives we share? The answer hangs in the balance as it has for generations. That is what makes our current efforts to understand and respond to this central issue in our common lives both necessary and important. Our hopes are in our own hands, in our own souls.

NOTES

1. AND THE POOR GET POORER (AND YOUNGER)

1. *Beyond the Myths* (Washington: Center on Social Welfare Policy and Law, 1992), p. iii.

2. Lee Rainwater, *What Money Buys* (New York: Basic Books, 1974) discusses how poverty makes it difficult for people to do everyday things in the same way as the rest of society.

3. There is a lesson to be learned here from rape crisis centers who use the term rape survivor rather than rape victim to reinforce the effort of rape survivors to regain control over their own lives as a central element of their recovery.

4. This is the task my theology of freedom and community addresses. See chapter 9.

5. The Children's Defense Fund is the most significant force outside of government pressing for changes in public policy aimed at poverty. The Fund merges passion with political savvy in pressing for a truly comprehensive approach to the needs of poor children.

6. The contrast between the political unpopularity of the National Welfare Rights Organization and the relative political success of the Children's Defense Fund is based in part in this ambiguity.

7. We shall return to this matter repeatedly as we think about the ethical question of human worth raised by poverty.

8. The statistics used in this book and especially in this chapter are drawn primarily from three sources: *Economic Report of the president: Transmitted to the Congress, February, 1992* (Washington: U.S. Government Printing Office, 1992); Subcommittee on Human Resources of the Committee on Ways and Means of the U.S. House of Representatives, *Sources of the Increases in Poverty, Work Effort, and Income Distribution Data* (Washington: U.S. Government Printing Office, 1993); Children's Defense Fund, *The State of America's Children: 1992* (Washington: Children's Defense Fund, 1992). These three resources are the official economic document of a Republican

president, an official document of the Democratic-controlled House Ways and Means Committee, and the basic yearly publication of the most significant advocacy group for the poor. They represent very different perspectives on poverty and welfare, and yet the basic numbers are essentially the same.

9. Children's Defense Fund, *The State of America's Children: 1992*, p. 31, contrasts generally held beliefs about welfare with facts.

10. This and other recent changes in welfare policy will be discussed in chapter 11.

11. Michael Harrington, *The New American Poverty* (New York: Viking Penquin, 1984), pp. 70-88, describes how this poverty standard developed and the recent debate over it. Also Stephen Sapp briefly describes the formula and the controversy in *Light on a Gray Area: American Public Policy on Aging*, Churches' Center for Public Policy Series (Nashville: Abingdon Press, 1992), pp. 53-54.

12. *Economic Report of the President: 1992*, pp. 143-44, raises this issue.

13. Harrington, *The New American Poverty*, pp. 77-88, makes this case.

14. Rainwater, *What Money Buys* addresses this in detail.

15. The following data are drawn from the same sources as the welfare facts were. See note 8.

16. Sapp, *Light on a Gray Area*, pp. 215-16, recognizes this reality in the context of a thorough discussion of the equally real problems of older Americans.

17. National Commission on America's Urban Families, *Families First* (Washington: U.S. Government Printing Office, 1993), p. 26.

18. Frank Levy, *Dollars and Dreams* (New York: Russell Sage, 1987) discusses in detail the effects of this lack of increase in wages.

19. Lester Thurow, *The Zero-Sum Solution* (New York: Simon and Schuster, 1985), pp. 60-66, discusses this trend more fully.

20. William Julius Wilson, *The Truly Disadvantaged* (Chicago: The University of Chicago Press, 1987) has this division as its essential thesis.

21. Frances Fox Piven and Richard A. Cloward, "The Contemporary Relief Debate," in Fred Block, et al., *The Mean Season* (New York: Random House, 1987), pp. 45-108, lay out these cuts.

22. Gunnar Myrdal, *An American Dilemma* (New York: Harper, 1944 and 1962), pp. 75-78, developed the concept of a vicious circle to describe how various factors contributed to racism in America. I am making a similar point here.

2. NOTHING NEW: THE HISTORY OF POVERTY AS A PUBLIC ISSUE IN THE UNITED STATES

1. Russell E. Smith and Dorothy Zietz, *American Welfare Institutions* (New York: John Wiley & Sons, 1970), p. 15.

2. Blanche Coll, *Perspectives in Public Welfare: A History* (Washington: U.S. Department of Health, Education, and Welfare, 1969) is the primary source for this history of welfare practices before this century.

3. Ibid., pp. 29-39.

4. Ibid., pp. 40-62.

5. The COS doctrine died hard. On the basis of it, the organized charities opposed the direct public assistance of the New Deal at first.

6. Frank B. Bruel, "Early History of Aid to the Unemployed in the United States," in *In Aid of the Unemployed,* ed. Joseph M. Becker (Baltimore: Johns Hopkins Press, 1965), p. 10.

7. Smith and Zietz, *American Welfare Institutions,* p. 39.

8. Robert Hunter, *Poverty* (New York: Macmillan, 1904).

9. Ibid., pp. 60-61.

10. Ibid., pp. 63-64.

11. Amos G. Warner, *American Charities* (New York: Thomas T. Crowell, 1894) is the best example of the mature COS position.

12. Robert Bremner, *Up from the Depths* (New York: New York University Press, 1956), pp. 131-35.

13. Much of this account of settlement houses is drawn from Allen F. Davis, *Spearheads for Reform* (New York: Oxford University Press, 1967) and Clarke A. Chambers, *Seedtime of Reform* (Minneapolis: University of Minnesota Press, 1963). The generalizations that follow are limited, as was the work of Davis, to those settlements most involved in social reform. These same settlements had the widest influence and publicity.

14. Bremner, *Up from the Depths,* pp. 128-39.

15. For accounts of the breadth and effectiveness of efforts at state legislation see Coll, *Perspectives in Public Welfare,* pp. 69-85, and Roy Lubove, *The Struggle for Social Security* (Cambridge: Harvard University Press, 1968).

16. This ambiguity is well represented in the contrast between Chambers, *Seedtime for Reform* and John Chamberlain, *Farewell to Reform* (New York: John Day Company, 1932).

17. In a sense the old COS approach was revived with psychological counseling replacing spiritual uplift.

18. Chambers, *Seedtime for Reform* and Lubove, *Struggle for Social Security* are particularly helpful on the activity of this time between eras of reform.

19. Searle F. Charles, *Minister of Relief* (Syracuse: Syracuse University Press, 1963), p. 237. Much of the subsequent discussion of Hopkins is informed by this book.

20. Robert E. Sherwood, *Roosevelt and Hopkins* (New York: Harper & Brothers, 1948), p. 84.

21. Paul K. Conkin, *FDR and the Origins of the Welfare State* (New York: Thomas Y. Crowell, 1967), p. 73.

22. Ibid., p. 64. Similar conclusions were shared by a number of authors writing in the early sixties. For a review of that literature, see Dwight Macdonald, "Books: Our Invisible Poor," *The New Yorker,* January 19, 1963, pp. 110-12. This review and the literature reviewed caught John F. Kennedy's attention.

23. Ibid., p. 23.

24. Maxwell S. Stewart, *Social Security* (New York: W.W. Norton, 1937), pp. 305-13, describes these state programs in detail.

25. Arthur Link, *An American Epoch* (New York: Knopf, 1955), p. 72, and Smith and Zietz, *American Welfare Institutions,* pp. 63-64. For an opposing view see Otis L. Graham, Jr., *An Encore for Reform* (New York: Oxford University Press, 1967). It seems

to me that much of this debate about whether or not the New Deal was the direct descendent of the Progressives fails to note the distinctions within each, which I have suggested. While I would recognize the discontinuity between them taken broadly, I would argue for a real continuity between the specific reform elements within each that I have discussed.

26. Lyndon Johnson, "Special Message to the Congress Proposing a Nationwide War on the Sources of Poverty: March 16, 1964," *Public Papers of the Presidents of the United States: Lyndon Johnson: 1963-64* (Washington: U.S. Government Printing Office, 1965), Book I, p. 380.

27. Elinor Graham, "The Politics of Poverty," in *The Great Society Reader,* ed. Marvin E. Gettleman and Davis Mermelstein (New York: Random House, 1967), pp. 213-30; Daniel Patrick Moynihan, "The Professionalization of Reform," in *The Great Society Reader,* pp. 459-75; and Peter Marris and Martin Rein, *Dilemmas of Social Reform* (London: Routledge and Kegan Paul, 1967), p. 1.

28. Much of my discussion of the origins of community action and of Mobilization for Youth is drawn from Marris and Rein, *Dilemmas of Social Reform.*

29. John Kenneth Galbraith, *The Affluent Society* (Boston: Houghton, Mifflin and Company, 1958).

30. Harry M. Caudill, *Night Comes to the Cumberland* (Boston: Little, Brown and Company, 1963).

31. Gabriel Kolko, *Wealth and Power in the United States* (New York: Preager, 1962).

32. Robert J. Lampman, *The Share of Top Wealthholders in National Wealth: 1922-1956* (Princeton: Princeton University Press, 1962).

33. Michael Harrington, *The Other America* (New York: The Macmillan Company, 1962).

34. Ben B. Seligman, *Poverty as a Public Issue* (New York: Free Press, 1965), p. 5; James L. Sundquist, *Politics and Policy* (Washington, D.C.: The Brookings Institution, 1968); and Moynihan, "The Professionalization of Reform" all discuss these pressures.

35. Macdonald, "Books: Our Invisible Poor."

36. Richard A. Cloward and Lloyd E. Ohlin, *Delinquency and Opportunity* (Glencoe, Ill.: The Free Press, 1960).

37. Ibid., p. 211.

38. Moynihan, "The Professionalization of Reform"; and Frances Fox Piven, "Politics and Planning," in *Justice and the Law in the Mobilization for Youth Experience,* ed. Harold H. Weissman (New York: Associated Press, 1969), pp. 167-91.

39. Piven, "Politics and Planning," pp. 183-85.

40. Ibid.

41. For a discussion of both this conflict theory and the reluctance of government officials to accept it, see Richard A. Cloward, "The War on Poverty—Are the Poor Left Out?" in *Poverty: Power and Politics,* ed. Chaim Isaac Waxman (New York: Grosset & Dunlap, 1968), pp. 159-70.

42. Marris and Rein, *Dilemmas of Social Reform,* pp.176-81.

43. Marris and Rein, *Dilemmas of Social Reform* has as its basic purpose laying out this confusion, or conflict, in understandings of community action. Daniel Patrick Moynihan does the same from his perspective in *Maximum Feasible Misunderstanding* (New York: The Free Press, 1969), pp. 56-57.

44. Moynihan, *Maximum Feasible Misunderstanding*, p. 131.

45. Marris and Rein, *Dilemmas of Social Reform*, pp. 89-91.

3. HOW THE POOR CAME TO GET WELFARE: THE HISTORY OF WELFARE POLICY IN THE UNITED STATES

1. This issue will be taken up primarily under the ethical question of human worth, which we shall consider in what follows.

2. No doubt this is due in part to the fact that older Americans vote in high percentages.

3. In recent years this funding has been increased in times of high unemployment so that benefits can be extended for additional months for those unable to find work.

4. Different states and localities also have a different range of benefits and tougher or easier administrative procedures.

5. In recent years state and local governments have faced tough budget problems so welfare benefits have been cut.

6. In recent years many states have reduced General Assistance; for instance, GA recipients in Ohio now can only receive benefits for six months in any year. Some states have eliminated it entirely.

7. For this reason we shall take up ethical questions as we examine various analyses of poverty and welfare.

8. Frances Fox Piven and Richard A. Cloward, *Regulating the Poor* (New York: Random House, 1971), p. 186.

9. Gilbert Y. Steiner, *The State of Welfare* (Washington: The Brookings Institution, 1971), p. 37.

10. Daniel Patrick Moynihan, *Family and Nation* (New York: Harcourt Brace Jovanovich, 1986), p. 117, discusses the thinking behind this.

11. Ibid., pp. 119-21.

12. According to Moynihan, this was the basis of Richard Nixon's support for the program. Ibid., p.122.

13. Steiner, *The State of Welfare*, p. 49.

14. Piven and Cloward, *Regulating the Poor*, p. 183.

15. The very name "Supplemental Security Income" suggests a small and appropriate program.

16. Daniel Patrick Moynihan, *The Politics of a Guaranteed Income* (New York: Random House, 1973), p. 184.

17. This is a central point of the famous interview of David Stockman in William Greider, "The Education of David Stockman," *The Atlantic Monthly*, 248 (December, 1981), pp. 29-30.

18. *Budget of the United States Government, Fiscal Year 1993* (Washington: U.S. Government Printing Office, 1992).

19. The classic description of the negative income tax is in Milton Friedman, *Capitalism and Freedom* (Chicago: University of Chicago Press, 1962), pp. 190-95.

20. I first saw a chart like this in Philip Wogaman, *Guaranteed Annual Income: The*

Moral Issues (Nashville: Abingdon Press, 1968), p. 29. This book remains the best previous discussion of the ethics of welfare policy.

21. Moynihan, *The Politics of a Guaranteed Income*, pp. 352-66, discusses how this led liberals to oppose Nixon's welfare reform proposal.

22. United States Congress: House Committee on Ways and Means, *Social Security and Welfare Proposals: Hearings before the Committee on Ways and Means* (Washington: U.S. Government Printing Office, 1970), Part 3, pp. 1013-39.

4. THE VIRTUE OF BEING POOR BUT INDEPENDENT: CHARLES MURRAY

1. Charles Murray, *Losing Ground* (New York: Basic Books, 1984).
2. Ibid., p. 29.
3. Ibid., pp. 16-20.
4. Ibid., pp. 22-23.
5. Ibid., p. 44.
6. Ibid., pp. 53-142. The results are summarized on pp. 135-42.
7. Ibid., p. 146.
8. Ibid., pp. 156-62.
9. Ibid., p. 161.
10. Ibid., pp. 162-65.
11. Ibid., pp. 167-77.
12. Ibid., pp. 178-91. Status is finally a moral term, society's way of rewarding behavior it believes is good.
13. Ibid., p. 185.
14. Once again, deserving is a moral category.
15. Ibid., p. 204.
16. Ibid., p. 211.
17. Ibid., p. 212.
18. Ibid., p. 216.
19. Ibid., p. 217.
20. Ibid., p. 218.
21. Ibid., p. 223.
22. Ibid., pp. 223-27.
23. Ibid., pp. 227-36.
24. Ibid., pp. 227-28.
25. Ibid., p. 233.
26. Ibid., p. 236.
27. Milton Friedman, *Capitalism and Freedom* (Chicago: University of Chicago Press, 1962) is the classic statement of Friedman's public philosophy and policy positions. Chapters 10, 11, and 12 (pp. 161-95) deal with his position on poverty and welfare.
28. Murray, *Losing Ground*, pp. 234-35.
29. Ibid., pp. 235.
30. Ibid., p. 234.
31. Ibid., p. 234.

32. Ibid., p. 146.
33. Ibid., p. 185.
34. Ibid.
35. Ibid., p. 177.

5. DEVELOPING COMPETENT PEOPLE: LISBETH SCHORR

1. Lisbeth B. Schorr, *Within Our Reach* (New York: Doubleday, 1988), pp. xx.
2. Ibid., p. xix.
3. Ibid.
4. Ibid., pp. xxii-xxiv.
5. Ibid., p. 288.
6. Ibid., pp. xxiv-xxvi.
7. Ibid., p. xxvi.
8. Ibid., p. xxviii.
9. Ibid., pp.17-18.
10. Ibid., p. 29.
11. Ibid., pp. 33-63.
12. Ibid., pp. 64-84.
13. Ibid., pp. 85-110.
14. Ibid., pp. 111-39.
15. Ibid., p. 139.
16. Ibid., pp. 140-78.
17. Ibid., pp. 179-214.
18. Ibid., pp. 191-92.
19. Ibid., pp. 215-55.
20. Ibid., p. 257.
21. Ibid., p. 259.
22. Ibid., pp. 263-64.
23. Ibid., p. 267.
24. Ibid., p. 288.
25. Ibid., p. xx.
26. Ibid., p. 270.

6. BEHAVING LIKE A GOOD POOR CITIZEN: LAWRENCE MEAD

1. In part because voters perceived that authoritarian conservatives had captured the Republican National Convention in 1992, George Bush could not hold the Reagan coalition together.

2. Wisconsin may be the best example; recent changes there take benefits away from people who do what the state does not want them to do, such as have more children or drop out of school.

3. Lawrence M. Mead, *Beyond Entitlement* (New York: The Free Press, 1986), p. ix.

199

4. Ibid., p. ix.
5. Ibid., p. 3.
6. This is Mead's version of what Murray calls the elite wisdom.
7. Ibid., p. 33.
8. Ibid., p. 70.
9. Ibid., p. 82.
10. Ibid., p. 87.
11. Ibid., pp. 104-11.
12. Ibid., p. 119.
13. Ibid., pp. 135-41.
14. Ibid., pp. 145-47.
15. Ibid., p. 151.
16. Ibid., p. 167.
17. Ibid., pp. 194-200.
18. Ibid., pp. 200-215.
19. Ibid., p. 215.
20. Ibid., p. 217.
21. Ibid., p. 219.
22. Ibid., p. 226.
23. Ibid., p. 229.
24. Ibid., p. 239.
25. Ibid., p. 240.
26. Ibid., pp. 242-43.
27. Ibid., p. 215.
28. Ibid., p. 88.
29. Ibid., pp. 88-89.
30. Ibid., p. 10.

7. STRUGGLING AGAINST AN UNJUST SYSTEM: FRANCES FOX PIVEN

1. Ohlin's move was described in chapter 2.
2. Frances Fox Piven and Richard A. Cloward, *Regulating the Poor* (New York: Random House, 1971).
3. Ibid., p. 3.
4. Ibid., pp. 45-119.
5. Ibid., pp. 200-221, discusses the factors that led up to the migration.
6. Ibid., pp. 222-47, describes what happened after migration.
7. Ibid., pp. 222-26.
8. Ibid., pp. 222-26, catalogues these factors that laid the groundwork for the Great Society.
9. Ibid., pp. 249-50.
10. Ibid., discusses the various elements in the War on Poverty which led to increases in the welfare rolls.
11. Ibid., pp. 337-38.
12. Ibid., p. 338.

13. Ibid., p. 345.

14. Ibid., p. 348.

15. Barbara Ehrenreich and Frances Fox Piven, "Women and the Welfare State, in *Alternatives: Proposals for America from the Democratic Left,* ed. Irving Howe (New York: Random House, 1984), p. 41-60.

16. Ibid.

17. Frances Fox Piven and Richard A. Cloward, "The Contemporary Relief Debate," in Fred Block, et al., *The Mean Season* (New York: Random House, 1987), pp. 45-108, is a good example of this response.

18. Frances Fox Piven and Richard A. Cloward, "The Historical Sources of the Contemporary Relief Debate," in *The Mean Season,* p. 7.

19. Ibid., pp. 7-8.

20. Piven and Cloward, "The Contemporary Relief Debate," p. 57.

21. Ibid., p. 96.

22. Frances Fox Piven and Richard A. Cloward, "Explaining the Politics of the Welfare State or Marching Back Toward Pluralism?" in *Beyond the Marketplace,* eds. Roger Friedland and A.F. Robertson (New York: Aldine de Gruyter, 1990), pp. 245-69, argues this throughout the history of welfare in the United States.

23. Richard A. Cloward and Frances Fox Piven, "Birth of a Movement," *The Nation,* 204 (May 8, 1967): 582-88, was an attempt to bring national exposure to the NWRO.

24. Ehrenreich and Piven, "The Feminization of Poverty," p. 127.

25. An example of this criticism is Robert B. Albritton, "Social Amelioration through Mass Insurgency?: A Reexamination of the Piven and Cloward Thesis," *American Political Science Review* (December 1979): 1003-11.

26. Piven and Cloward, "The Contemporary Relief Debate," p. 98.

27. Ibid., pp. 100-101.

8. WORLD VIEWS, THEOLOGIES, AND SOCIAL ETHICS

1. Charles Murray, *Losing Ground* (New York: Basic Books, 1984), pp. 157-58.

2. Frances Fox Piven and Richard A. Cloward, "The Contemporary Relief Debate," in Fred Block, et al., *The Mean Season* (New York: Random House, 1987), p. 96.

3. Ibid.

4. Much of this use of Aristotle is based upon the work of one of the great scholars of Aristotle of our time, Richard McKeon. See Richard McKeon, *Freedom and History* (New York: Noonday Press, 1952) and especially "Philosophy and Action," *Ethics* 62 (January, 1952): 79-100.

5. This distinction is one I was introduced to by W. Alvin Pitcher. For a similar analysis see W. Alvin Pitcher, "Radically Different Approaches to Foreign Policy," *Chicago Theological Seminary Register* 50 (April 1960): 22-26.

6. Max Weber, *The Protestant Ethic and the Spirit of Capitalism,* trans. Talcott Parsons (New York: Charles Scribner's Sons, 1958).

7. For instance, see Alan Simpson, *Puritanism in Old and New England* (Chicago: University of Chicago Press, 1955), pp. 19-38.

8. Martin E. Marty, *Righteous Empire* (New York: Dial Press, 1970), pp. 46-56, provides a brief discussion of this shift. A more detailed treatment is Nathan O. Hatch, *The Democratization of American Christianity* (New Haven: Yale University Press, 1989).

9. Andrew Carnegie, *The Gospel of Wealth and Other Essays* (New York: Andrew Carnegie, 1933) may be the purest expression of the developed form of this ethic.

10. For instance, see Jerry Falwell, *Listen, America!* (New York: Doubleday, 1980), pp. 59-70.

11. National Conference of Catholic Bishops, *Economic Justice for All* (Washington: United States Catholic Conference, 1986) is an example of the more dynamic view. It still has a less dynamic view of reality than I do; see Warren R. Copeland, *Economic Justice* (Nashville: Abingdon, 1988), pp. 125-47.

12. Robert Benne, *The Ethic of Democratic Capitalism* (Philadelphia: Fortress, 1981) is a good example of the Lutheran approach, which touches upon the issues of poverty and welfare.

13. Erling Jorstad, *The Politics of Moralism* (Minneapolis: Augsburg, 1981) stresses this aspect of the new religious right. Nancy T. Ammerman, "North American Protestant Fundamentalism," in *Fundamentalisms Observed*, Martin E. Marty and R. Scott Appleby, ed. (Chicago: University of Chicago Press, 1991), pp. 45-49, sees the family issue as key.

14. Falwell, *Listen, America!*, pp. 104-18.

15. Gustavo Gutiérrez, *A Theology of Liberation*, trans. and ed. Sister Caridad Inda and John Eagleson (Maryknoll, N.Y.: Orbis, 1973).

16. James Luther Adams, *On Being Human Religiously*, ed. Max L. Stackhouse (Boston: Beacon, 1976), p. 93.

17. Marian Wright Edelman, *The Measure of Our Success* (Boston: Beacon, 1992), pp. 78.

18. Ibid., p. 86.

19. Marian Wright Edelman in The Children's Defense Fund, *The State of America's Children: 1992* (Washington: Children's Defense Fund, 1992), p. xxi.

20. Edelman, *The Measure of Our Success*, pp. 37-78.

9. A THEOLOGY OF FREEDOM AND COMMUNITY

1. I begin with Warren Copeland not because he is particularly important or particularly relevant to the topic of this book, but simply because his experience is what I know best. In so doing, I follow Whitehead, for example Alfred North Whitehead, *Adventures of Ideas* (New York: Macmillan, 1933), pp. 220-21. This is the work by Whitehead I shall draw upon the most in constructing this theology. The page numbers are from the Free Press Edition.

2. Ibid., pp. 175-90.

3. Ibid., pp. 191-200.

4. Ibid., p. 179.

5. Alfred North Whitehead, *Process and Reality* (New York: Macmillan, 1929), pp. 403-13, is Whitehead's most extended discussion of the relation between God and the world. Page numbers are from The Free Press edition.

6. Whitehead, *Adventures of Ideas.*

7. Ibid., pp. 69-70.

8. Ibid., p. 6.

9. Ibid., p. 69.

10. Two good resources for relating process thought to social ethics are Lois Gehr Livezey, "Rights, Goods, and Virtues: Toward an Interpretation of Justice in Process Thought," *The Annual of the Society of Christian Ethics: 1986* (Knoxville, Tenn.: Society of Christian Ethics, 1986), pp. 37-64; and John B. Cobb, Jr., and W. Widick Schroeder, *Process Philosophy and Social Thought* (Chicago: Center for the Scientific Study of Religion, 1981).

11. Two good resources on the relation between process thought and Christian theology which are readable by beginners are John B. Cobb, Jr., and David Ray Griffin, *Process Theology: An Introductory Exposition* (Philadelphia: Westminster Press, 1976) and Marjorie Hewitt Suchocki, *God, Christ, Church* (New York: Crossroad, 1988). A good resource at a more sophisticated level is *Process Philosophy and Christian Thought,* Delwin Brown, Ralph E. James, Jr., and Gene Reeves, eds. (Indianapolis: Bobbs-Merrill, 1971).

12. Livezey, "Rights, Goods, and Virtues," describes Whitehead's attempt to establish the reality of choice in the flow of events.

13. Bernard Loomer, "Theology in the American Grain," in Cobb and Schroeder, *Process Thought and Political Theory,* develops the concept of community in process thought.

14. James Luther Adams, *On Being Human Religiously,* ed. Max L. Stackhouse (Boston: Beacon, 1976), pp. 97-99.

15. Most contemporary ethicists who stress sin refer to Reinhold Niebuhr. Ruth Smith, "Feminism and the Moral Subject," in *Women's Consciousness, Women's Conscience,* ed. Barbara Hilkert Andolsen, Christine E. Gudorf and Mary D. Pellauer (New York: Harper & Row, 1985), pp. 235-50, responds to Niebuhr in a way consistent with my discussion here.

16. Whitehead, *Adventures of Ideas,* pp. 10-26.

10. UNDERSTANDING THE HUMAN MEANING OF POVERTY: WILLIAM JULIUS WILSON AND BEYOND

1. These two lines from the poem "The New Colossus," written by Emma Lazarus in 1883 to raise money for the Statue of Liberty, are placed at its base.

2. Michael Harrington, *The New American Poverty* (New York: Holt, Rinehart and Winston, 1984), pp. 1-13.

3. Charles Murray, *Losing Ground* (New York: Basic Books, 1984), pp. 53-68; and Lawrence M. Mead, *Beyond Entitlement* (New York: The Free Press, 1986), pp. 18-25.

4. William Julius Wilson, *The Truly Disadvantaged* (Chicago: University of Chicago Press, 1987).

5. Ibid., pp. 21-29.

6. Ibid., pp. 29-46.

7. Ibid., pp. 46-62 is the entire discussion of the concentration effect.

8. Ibid., pp. 66-71.

9. Ibid., pp. 81-92.

10. Ibid., pp. 77-81.

11. William Julius Wilson, *The Declining Significance of Race* (Chicago: The University of Chicago Press, 1978).

12. Wilson, *The Truly Disadvantaged*, pp. 112-18, contains the discussion of all three principles.

13. A good example of this criticism is E. R. Ricketts and I. V. Sawhill, *Defining and Measuring the Underclass* (Washington: The Urban Institute, 1986).

14. Wilson, *The Truly Disadvantaged*, pp. 182-83.

15. Murray, *Losing Ground*, p. 162.

16. Mead, *Beyond Entitlement*, pp. 79-82.

17. Harrington, *The New American Poverty*, pp. 202-6.

18. Wilson, *The Truly Disadvantaged*, pp. 14-15.

19. Richard A. Cloward and Lloyd E. Ohlin, *Delinquency and Opportunity* (Glencoe, Ill.: The Free Press, 1960), which was discussed in more detail in chapter 2, is a classic statement of this view.

20. Lisbeth B. Schorr, *Within Our Reach* (New York: Doubleday, 1988), p. xx.

21. Frances Fox Piven and Richard A. Cloward, "The Contemporary Relief Debate," in Fred Block, et al. *The Mean Season* (New York: Random House, 1987), pp. 96-101.

22. Elliot Liebow, *Tally's Corner* (Boston: Little, Brown and Company, 1967).

23. Hyman Rodman, "The Lower-Class Value Stretch," *Social Forces* 62, No. 2 (December, 1963): 205-15.

24. Wilson, *The Truly Disadvantaged*, p. 138.

25. Murray, *Losing Ground*, p. 186.

26. In fact, Whitehead criticizes what he calls the literary understanding of freedom, which does not take seriously the problems of having the effective capacity to choose, including the economic wherewithal. Alfred North Whitehead, *Adventures of Ideas* (New York: Macmillan, 1933), pp. 65-68.

27. Hannah Arendt, *On Revolution* (Viking Compass Edition: New York: The Viking Press, 1965), p. 54. Much of this discussion of the human meaning of poverty is dependent upon Arendt.

11. THE WELFARE REFORM WARS: DANIEL PATRICK MOYNIHAN AND BEYOND

1. Daniel Patrick Moynihan, *Maximum Feasible Misunderstanding* (New York: The Free Press, 1969) is his reflections on the War on Poverty.

2. That debate is represented well in Lee Rainwater, *The Moynihan Report and the Politics of Controversy* (Cambridge: M.I.T. Press, 1967); and William Ryan, *Blaming the Victim* (New York: Pantheon, 1971).

3. Daniel P. Moynihan, *The Politics of a Guaranteed Income* (New York: Random House, 1973), pp. 17-26.

4. This is when he wrote *Maximum Feasible Misunderstanding.*

5. Frances Fox Piven, "The Demonstration Project: A Federal Strategy for Local Change," in *Justice and the Law in the Mobilization for Youth Experience,* ed. Harold H. Weissman (New York: Associated Press, 1969).

6. Moynihan, *The Politics of a Guaranteed Income* is his story of this attempt at welfare reform.

7. Ibid., pp. 179-94.

8. Ibid., pp. 229-35, lays out the specifics of the proposal.

9. Ibid., pp. 236-347, discusses all of the various public reactions.

10. Daniel Patrick Moynihan, *Family and Nation* (New York: Harcourt Brace Jovanovich, 1986) provides his rationale for recent legislation.

11. Barbara R. Bergman, "A Fresh Start on Welfare Reform," *Challenge* (November-December, 1987), pp. 44-50.

12. Charles Murray, *Losing Ground* (New York: Basic Books, 1984), p. 233.

13. Milton Friedman, *Capitalism and Freedom* (Chicago: University of Chicago Press, 1962), p. 191. The majority can agree to eliminate the program if it wants, and benefit levels depend on how much taxes the electorate is willing to pay to support it.

14. Whether we are antagonistic toward the poor or feel sorry for them, we are not accepting them as fellow human beings and citizens.

15. Lawrence Mead, *Beyond Entitlement* (New York: The Free Press, 1986), p. 256, is very direct about this need for conformity.

16. Pamela D. Couture, *Blessed Are the Poor?* (Nashville: Abingdon, 1991) is an excellent treatment of this entire issue focused on how it affects women who are poor.

17. Mead, *Beyond Entitlement,* pp. 152-68, recognizes the problem and proposes measures to improve morale among work requirement enforcers.

18. This disparity has been growing lately as public services deteriorate and more people turn to private services to replace them.

19. Schorr, *Within Our Reach,* p. 258.

20. This is the main point of Daniel Patrick Moynihan, "The Professionalization of Reform," in *The Great Society Reader,* ed. Marvin E. Gettleman and Davis Mermelstein (New York: Random House, 1967).

21. Charles Murray, *Losing Ground* (New York: Basic Books, 1984), pp. 176-77.

22. Schorr, *Within Our Reach,* pp. 1-22, describes these costs well.

23. This division is the basic point of William Julius Wilson, *The Truly Disadvantaged* (Chicago: The University of Chicago Press, 1987).

12. WHERE DO WE GO FROM HERE? BILL CLINTON AND BEYOND

1. Martin Luther King, Jr., *Where Do We Go from Here?: Chaos or Community?* (New York: Harper & Row, 1967).

2. Ibid., p. 162.

3. Ronald Reagan often criticized the entire civil rights movement for straying from their original purpose.

4. Ross Perot appeals directly to this belief among Americans.

5. John Cobb and Herman Daly, *For the Common Good* (Boston: Beacon Press, 1989) is the best-known statement of the latest attack on economic growth. They argue for rethinking our whole concept of economic growth in terms of what economic goods really serve the human good.

6. Lester C. Thurow, *The Zero-Sum Society* (New York: Simon and Schuster, 1985) is a good example of this approach.

7. Robert Z. Lawrence, *Can America Compete?* (Washington, D.C.: Brookings, 1984) is a good statement of this view.

8. He proposes a hidden agenda that addresses full employment and other issues which would be particularly helpful to African Americans without ever mentioning race. William Julius Wilson, *The Truly Disadvantaged* (Chicago: The University of Chicago Press, 1987), pp. 140-64.

9. Only metropolitan racial and economic integration can overcome these divisions but that is not a real political possibility at this point.

10. Gretchen Reynolds, "The Rising Significance of Race," *Chicago* (December, 1992), pp. 81-85 and 126-30, lays out the parallels between Wilson and Clinton.

11. Gwen Ifill, "Clinton Presses Welfare Overhaul," *New York Times* (September 10, 1992), Section A, pp. 1, 20.

12. The State of Ohio, for instance, passed cuts that allowed General Assistance recipients to receive benefits for only six months at a time after which they had to wait six months to apply again.

13. The female reference is intentional here because it is almost always women who are the single parents with children, especially among the poor.

14. For instance, Senator Russell B. Long of Louisiana was one of the most adamant and powerful opponents of welfare reform but was key in introducing and expanding the Earned Income Tax Credit.

15. Selma Fraiberg, *Every Child's Birthright* (New York: Bantam, 1978) argues strongly for mothers staying home.

16. This is exactly the position of the Children's Defense Fund, which supports work opportunities and supportive services for working mothers.

17. Hillary Rodham Clinton has served on the Board of the Children's Defense Fund, and one of the first appearances of the Clintons in Washington after the election was at a Fund event.

18. Two classic sources for this view of social change are John Dewey, *The Public and Its Problems* (New York: Henry Holt and Company, 1927); and James Luther Adams, *Voluntary Associations*, ed. J. Ronald Engel (Chicago: Exploration Press, 1986).

19. Marian Wright Edelman, *The Measure of Our Success* (Boston: Beacon Press, 1992), pp. 93-94.

20. Ibid., p. 94.

SUGGESTIONS FOR FURTHER READING

INFORMATION ON POVERTY AND WELFARE
IN THE UNITED STATES

1. Center on Social Welfare Policy and Law. *Beyond the Myths.* Washington: Center on Social Welfare Policy and Law, 1992.
2. Children's Defense Fund. *The State of America's Children: 1992.* Washington: Children's Defense Fund, 1992.
3. *Economic Report of the President: Transmitted to the Congress, February, 1992.* Washington: U.S. Government Printing Office, 1992.
4. Levy, Frank. *Dollars and Dreams.* New York: Russell Sage, 1987.
5. National Commission on America's Urban Families. *Families First.* Washington: U.S. Government Printing Office, 1993.
6. Subcommittee on Human Resources of the Committee on Ways and Means of the U.S, House of Representatives. *Sources of the Increase in Poverty, Work Effort, and Income Support Data.* Washington: U.S. Government Printing Office, 1993.

HISTORY OF POVERTY AND WELFARE
AS A PUBLIC ISSUE IN THE U.S.

Before the Twentieth Century

1. Coll, Blanche. *Perspectives in Public Welfare: A History.* Washington: U.S. Department of Health, Education, and Welfare, 1969.
2. Smith, Russell E., and Dorothy Zietz. *American Welfare Institutions.* New York: John Wiley & Sons, 1970.

The Progressive Era

1. Bremner, Robert. *Up From the Depths.* New York: New York University Press, 1956.
2. Chambers, Clarke A. *Seedtime of Reform.* Minneapolis: University of Minnesota Press, 1963.
3. Davis, Allen F. *Spearheads for Reform.* New York: Oxford University Press, 1967.
4. Lubove, Roy. *The Struggle for Social Security.* Cambridge: Harvard University Press, 1968.

The New Deal

1. Charles, Searle F. *Minister of Relief.* Syracuse: Syracuse University Press, 1963.
2. Conkin, Paul K. *FDR and the Origins of the Welfare State.* New York: Thomas Y. Crowell, 1967.
3. Sherwood, Robert E. *Roosevelt and Hopkins.* New York: Harper and Bros., 1948.

The Great Society

1. Cloward, Richard A., and Lloyd E. Ohlin. *Delinquency and Opportunity.* Glencoe, Ill.: The Free Press, 1960.
2. Harrington, Michael. *The Other America.* New York: Macmillan,
3. Marris, Peter and Martin Rein. *Dilemmas of Social Reform.* London: Routledge and Kegan Paul, 1967.
4. Moynihan, Daniel Patrick. *Maximum Feasible Misunderstanding.* New York: The Free Press, 1969.

Recent Developments

1. Steiner, Gilbert Y. *The State of Welfare.* Washington: The Brookings Institution, 1973.
2. Moynihan, Daniel Patrick. *Family and Nation.* New York: Harcourt Brace Jovanovich, 1986.
3. ———. *The Politics of a Guaranteed Income.* New York: Random House, 1973.

ALTERNATIVE VIEWS OF POVERTY AND WELFARE

1. Ehrenreich, Barbara, and Francis Fox Piven. "Women and the Welfare State". In Irving Howe, ed. *Alternatives: Proposals for America from the Democratic Left.* New York: Random House, 1984.
2. Mead, Lawrence M. *Beyond Entitlement.* New York: The Free Press, 1986.
3. Murray, Charles. *Losing Ground.* New York: Basic Books, 1984.
4. Frances Fox, Piven, and Richard A. Cloward. "The Contemporary Relief Debate". In Fred Block, et. al. *The Mean Season.* New York: Random House, 1987.
5. ——— "The Historical Sources of the Contemporary Relief Debate." in Fred Bock, et. al. *The Mean Season.* New York: Random House, 1987.
6. ———. *Regulating the Poor.* New York: Random House, 1971.
7. Schorr, Lisbeth B. *Within Our Reach.* New York: Doubleday, 1988.

THEOLOGIES

Analytic Framework

1. McKeon, Richard. *Freedom and History.* New York: Noonday Press, 1952.

Alternative Theologies

1. Robert Benne. *The Ethic of Democratic Capitalism.* Philadelphia: Fortress, 1981.
2. Carnegie, Andrew. *The Gospel of Wealth and Other Essays.* New York: Andrew Carnegie, 1933.
3. Falwell, Jerry. *Listen America!* New York: Doubleday, 1980.
4. Gutiérrez, Gustavo. *A Theology of Liberation.* Maryknoll, N.Y.: Orbis, 1973.
5. Hatch, Nathan O. *The Democratization of American Christianity.* New Haven: Yale University Press, 1989.
6. National Conference of Catholic Bishops, *Economic Justice for All.* Washington: United States Catholic Conference, 1986.

Process Thought—Classic Sources

1. Whitehead, Alfred North. *Adventures of Ideas.* New York: Macmillan, 1933.
2. ———. *Process and Reality.* New York: Macmillan, 1929.

Process Thought and Christian Theology

1. Brown, Delwin, Ralph E. James, Jr., and Gene Reeves, eds. *Process Philosophy and Christian Thought.* Indianapolis: Bobbs-Merrill, 1971.
2. Cobb, B. Jr., and David Ray Griffin. *Process Theology: An Introductory Exposition.* Philadelphia: Westminster, 1976.
3. Suchocki, Marjorie Hewitt. *God, Christ, Church.* New York: Crossroad, 1988.

Process Thought and Social Ethics

1. Cobb, John B. Jr., and W. Widick Schroeder, eds. *Process Philosophy and Social Thought.* Chicago: Center for the Scientific Study of Religion, 1981.
2. Livezey, Lois Gehr. "Rights, Goods, and Virtues: Toward an Interpretation of Justice in Process Thought" in *The Annual of the Society of Christian Ethics: 1986.* Knoxville, Tenn.: Society of Christian Ethics, 1986.

THE DEEPER MEANING OF POVERTY AND WELFARE

1. Arendt, Hannah. *On Revolution.* New York: Viking, 1965.
2. Friedman, Milton. *Capitalism and Freedom.* Chicago: University of Chicago Press, 1962.
3. Harrington, Michael. *The New Poverty.* New York: Holt, Rinehart and Winston, 1984.

4. Liebow, Elliott. *Tally's Corner*. Boston: Little, Brown and Company, 1967.
5. ———. *The Moynihan Report and The Politics of Controversy*. Cambridge: M.I.T. Press, 1967.
6. Rainwater, Lee. *What Money Buys*. New York: Basic Books, 1974.
7. Rodman, Hyman. "The Lower-Class Value Stretch." In *Social Forces* 62, no. 2 (December, 1963): 205-215.
8. Ryan, William. *Blaming the Victim*. New York: Pantheon, 1971.

FUTURE POLICY

1. Adams, James Luther. *Voluntary Associations*. Edited by J. Ronald Engel. Chicago: Exploration Press, 1986.
2. Couture, Pamela. *Blessed Are the Poor? Woman's Poverty, Family Policy, and Practical Theology*. Nashville: Abingdon Press, 1991.
3. Dewey, John. *The Public and Its Problems*. New York: Henry Holt and Company, 1927.
4. ———. *Families in Peril*. Cambridge: Harvard University Press, 1987.
5. Edelman, Marian Wright. *The Measure of Our Success*. Boston: Beacon, 1992.
6. Sapp, Stephen, *Light on a Gray Area: American Public Policy and Aging*. Nashville: Abingdon Press, 1992.
7. Wogaman, Philip. *Guaranteed Annual Income: The Moral Issues*. Nashville: Abingdon Press, 1968.